Max-e-Marketing
in the
Net Future

Max-e-Marketing in the Net Future

The Seven Imperatives for Outsmarting the Competition in the Net Economy

Stan Rapp
Chuck Martin

McGraw-Hill

New York • San Francisco • Washington, D.C. • Auckland • Bogotá
Caracas • Lisbon • London • Madrid • Mexico City • Milan
Montreal • New Delhi • San Juan • Singapore
Sydney • Tokyo • Toronto

Library of Congress Cataloging-in-Publication Data

McGraw-Hill

*A Division of The **McGraw·Hill** Companies*

1 2 3 4 5 6 7 8 9 0 DOC/DOC 0 6 5 4 3 2 1 0

ISBN 0-07-136472-2

Printed and bound by R. R. Donnelley & Sons Company.

The Future Value Model is a trademark of McCann-Erickson WorldGroup.

This publication is designed to provide accurate and authoritative information in regard to the subject matter covered. It is sold with the understanding that neither the author nor the publisher is engaged in rendering legal, accounting, or other professional service. If legal advice or other expert assistance is required, the services of a competent professional person should be sought.

—From a Declaration of Principles jointly adopted by a Committee of the American Bar Association and a Committee of Publishers

McGraw-Hill books are available at special quantity discounts to use as premiums and sales promotions, or for use in corporate training programs. For more information, please write to the Director of Special Sales, Professional Publishing, McGraw-Hill, Two Penn Plaza, New York, NY 10121-2298. Or contact your local bookstore.

 This book is printed on recycled, acid-free paper containing a minimum of 50% recycled de-inked fiber.

To Jennifer and Grant, masters of the Net Future universe.

Stan Rapp

To Teri, Ryan, and Chase, who add true perspective to the Net Future.

Chuck Martin

Contents

Preface

The overwhelming reality of our time is not how much is changing; it's the overwhelming pace of change itself.

The transformation sweeping across the business scene in every country on every continent, rather than slowing and providing a breathing space, continues to quicken. Before there's time to respond to the latest "new thing," it's time to face what's coming next.

- What do you do when fortunes are made by people at companies that can't seem to make a profit?

- What do you do when some of those fortunes are wiped out in the blink of an eye?

- What do you do when reliance on mass marketing is replaced by selling to a segment of one?

- What do you do when the time-honored approach to building brand equity changes dramatically?

- What do you do when pricing power passes from the hands of the seller to the wish of the buyer?

- What do you do when fierce competitors strike up partnerships and even begin selling each other's products?

- What do you do when you are pulled one way by the "old economy" and another by the "new economy"?

To begin with, it helps to get real. There is only one economy that matters. It's the real economy of the Net Future—an economy that is driven by a startling new reality.

Soon, just about everyone in the twenty-first century—everywhere in the world—will be connected without wires to every thing and anyone from any place you are to anywhere you want to go or whatever you want to know. There are more than 500 million people on the planet already connected to the Internet, with its ranks growing exponentially.

When everyone can communicate easily and inexpensively with everyone else, the restricted communication channels that once controlled who knew what and when melt away. In this new environment, strategic thinking must be fundamentally restructured and new rules of competitive advantage are taking form for small and big businesses alike.

In Chuck Martin's 1999 best seller, *Net Future*, a spotlight was turned on those executives in business who get it and those who don't:[1]

> "The new fault line is between businesses that operate only in the bricks-and-mortar realm—such as many manufacturing entities and retailers—and businesses that operate in an online, interactive environment, such as online travel agents and CD retailers. In the Net Future, these two worlds will converge, as companies in each one begin to embrace the other."

Just a few months after Net Future appeared throughout the world, the smartest, established companies began pouring tens and hundreds of millions of dollars into e-marketing initiatives aimed at protecting its turf from the new kids on the block. The likely winners in the networked future understand that the new hybrid online/physical business will be driven in coming decades by the interactive digital component, not the traditional component.

Our purpose in writing this book is to make the unfamiliar forces driving success and failure in an uncertain world into a powerful ally rather than a shadow overhanging each step a company takes. It's about understanding the next phase of the turbulent Net Future. It's about seeing the new marketing as an evolutionary outgrowth of the individualized marketing approach that many smart marketers began to embrace in the 1980s and 1990s.

The rush to the Internet is accelerating the shift from mass marketing to the interactive marketing first heralded in the pages of *MaxiMarketing*, the book Stan Rapp and Tom Collins wrote almost a generation ago. The wonderful World Wide Web provides a tremendous new "booster engine" for targeting, acquiring, and keeping customers— and doing it more effectively and at lower cost than ever possible before.

MaxiMarketing was first published in 1986. Think how different it was then. The personal computer was only a few years old and struggling to catch on. Apple's Macintosh was looked upon by the business world as little more than a quaint toy with funny little icons instead of businesslike commands. There were relatively few fax machines, almost no e-mail, and today's ubiquitous mobile phone was a new idea on the horizon. Nobody had a clue that the Information Age was about to become the Mobile Information Age.

It was a time when the cost of accumulating, accessing, and analyzing customer data began to drop at an ever-increasing rate. Reluctantly at first, and then with growing excitement, managers looked down the long barrel of the distribution chain to discover the benefits of addressing known prospects and end users directly. But this new way of maximizing sales and profits by moving interactive customer relationships into a primary role remained a strongly resisted idea. It was the absolute opposite of the commonly held mass marketing and mass advertising wisdom of the time.

The feasibility of dealing on an addressable basis with known end users of a product or service had been the exclusive province of catalogue and subscription promotion direct marketers. But with increasing sophistication in the use of customer data and with the plummeting cost of managing the data, "being direct" no longer was the exclusive province of direct marketers. The MaxiMarketing concept spread steadily from the travel industry's frequent user loyalty programs, to every sector of financial services, to Dell Computer's transformation of the personal computer industry, and into the packaged goods arena for pet food, baby products, and other categories.

Then, almost overnight at the start of the twenty-first century, that info-tech software took MaxiMarketing to new heights of customer involvement and interaction. The rush to the Web opened unlimited vistas of personalization and customization. It made possible an affordable truly responsive relationship, continually refined in real time with end-user consumers and business-to-business customers.

We call this emerging new discipline *Max-e-Marketing in the Net Future*. It grows out of the continuing research of

Chuck Martin's team at the Net Future Institute and Stan Rapp's most recent years of experience as Chairman and CEO of McCann Relationship Marketing (MRM) Worldwide.

MRM is the relationship marketing services network—with offices in 46 countries—of McCann-Erickson World-Group, the world's no.1 global advertising agency. Rapp also serves on the Board of Directors of Net start-up Aveo and Net customer-care innovator iSKY as well as on the Board of Advisors of Naviant, the leader in outsourced member registration and targeted list compilation on the Net.

The Net Future Institute is a U.S.–based think tank, focusing on the future of e-business and the Internet. It comprises more than 3000 members from more than 1500 companies in 53 countries, and conducts regular surveys of those members, all of whom are personally invited to join. More than half are in senior managerial positions and half of the *Fortune 100* companies have at least one member. Martin also is on the Board of Directors of Handshake Dynamics, a leading strategic e-business consulting firm, and is on the Board of Advisors for Enamics. He lectures, advises companies, and conducts seminars around the world for some of the best and best-known companies in the world.

Max-e-Marketing is the wave of the future because it enables a company to achieve the kind of profitable customer relationships that simply were not possible before. At a time when business practices change at the speed of light, gaining the ultimate competitive advantage comes down to moving the fastest and being the smartest at taking advantage of the new rules of engagement. You may hear over and over that "the old rules don't apply in the New Economy" but you hear very little about what rules do apply.

Max-e-Marketing in the Net Future will *not* give you a magic formula for marketing success. What it will do is put a spotlight on the twists and turns the authors have identified along the road to e-marketing supremacy in the first decade of the new century and the new economy. They distill their considerable experience to spell out the Seven Marketing Imperatives you can follow to come out ahead in today's wildly competitive marketing arena. Informative interviews with some of the most innovative business leaders, who are shaping the direction of the new marketing, illustrate each concept.

In sharing their insights, the authors cover almost the entire business spectrum. Most of the references cited may not be from your particular business category. And many will not be from your geographical part of the world. It doesn't matter. The Max-e-Marketing Imperatives presented here have universal application—whether you're an e-commerce start-up or a retailer selling both online and offline—whether you manufacture a product, deliver a service, or play a vital role in the distribution chain—and whether you are doing business in Asia, Europe, or the Americas.

In the twentieth century, marketing was basically at the end of the value chain. Often a product was conceived, designed, manufactured, and started down the distribution channel before serious attention turned to marketing and promotion. In the Net economy, marketing moves up the value chain to the beginning of the process. Marketing drives the future value of the enterprise. Everyone within the organization now becomes a critical partner in carrying out the customer-centric marketing programs.

The biggest issue faced by every e-marketer is how to apply and adapt the new Max-e-Marketing Imperatives at every level of the organization—whether as an e-commerce start-up or a long-established global corporate enterprise dipping its giant toe into the digital marketing pond.

There is no escaping the challenges posed by the networked, global economy with its whole new world of opportunities—and pitfalls.

Welcome to Max-e-Marketing in the Net Future!

Stan Rapp
Chuck Martin

END NOTE

[1] From Chuck Martin , *Net Future*, (New York:; 1999; McGraw-Hill, 1999.)

Acknowledgments

While researching and writing this book, many people contributed both directly and indirectly along the way; we are very grateful to all of them.

Stan and Chuck have several people they want to thank, both together and individually.

We both are indebted to all the executives who spent their valuable time sharing their considerable insights and experiences. Without them, this book would not have been possible. To them, many, many thanks.

We also want to thank the 3000 Net Future Institute members, who are located in 53 countries and who regularly and thoughtfully answered our surveys and inquiries about the future of e-business and the Internet. Much of that primary research is used throughout the book.

A very special thank you goes to Mary Frakes, an established editor and journalist and long-time colleague and friend of Chuck, who worked with us to help craft the messages and honor the deadlines.

We would like to thank Iona Evans, former Director of Marketing and Research at the Institute, for not only conducting the Net Future Institute research, but also for helping in every research aspect of the book, including creating the URL index. We also want to thank Josh Jarvis, Director of Marketing and Research at the Net Future Institute, for global research and fact checking, Curran Osenton for research, and Katie Berry for help in proof-reading the final manuscript.

We want to thank Laurence Bunin at Handshake Dynamics for brainstorming on new business models and Steve Larsen at Net Perceptions for help in creating scenarios of how new technologies will be used.

Thanks to all our friends at McGraw-Hill—to Publisher Phil Ruppel, for putting Stan and Chuck together, to Senior Editor Mary Glenn for help and guidance all along the way, and to Ruth Mannino, Senior Editing Supervisor, who managed the manuscript through a challenging production schedule.

Stan would like to thank Patricia Berns, Director of Strategic Service, North America for MRM Worldwide, and Joanna Seddon, Director Brand Valuation of FutureBrand for taking the concept of measuring and leveraging the value of the customer relationship from the theoretical to the tested and proven MRM Future Value Model. Thanks also go to his many other skilled associates at McCann-Erickson WorldGroup.

As always for Stan, the support of his nearest and dearest is what makes everything possible. Special thanks at this time to Jennifer and Grant as they move into shaping their own very special future.

Chuck would like to thank the many great agents of the Leigh Speakers Bureau for introductions to the best companies and organizations in the world as a continuous and real-time learning experience.

A special thank you from Chuck goes to invaluable assistant Sarah Coito, who not only kept everything running on schedule, but also seemed to continually "create" time for Chuck to work on the book. He also would like to thank Don Tapscott, Richard Schroth, and David Ticoll for thoughtful ideas and continual support.

Chuck's biggest acknowledgment goes to his family, Teri, 11-year-old Ryan, and 9-year-old Chase, whose total support, understanding, and patience made this book possible.

Stan and Chuck

New Millennium! New Networked Economy! New Marketing Imperatives!

Decisions. Decisions. Decisions. More products to choose from. New ways to shop. Not enough time. Bombarded by commercial messages. Disappointed by customer service. The plight of the consumer of the new millennium.

New pressures to the bottom line. Internet buzz attacking the brand. The networking of everything. Shorter product life cycles. New expectations from savvy consumers. The plight of the businessperson of the new millennium.

As companies and their competition struggle to figure out how to adapt, survive, and prosper in an interconnected business world, one thing is clear. The interaction between an e-business and its e-customers will be radically different from anything ever seen before.

This new dynamic requires a new kind of link between a company and its customers, between the company and its stakeholders, between the brand perception and the brand experience—even between the company and its competitors. Forging these new connections will not be easy. The profound impact of the Internet on how modern-day society functions is destined to change marketing just as profoundly.

The wastefulness built into the mass marketing of the past is giving way to a newly affordable ability to communicate directly with the best prospects and customers. Fifty years of marketing orthodoxy has been turned on its head.

We've moved from mass marketing, to segmented marketing, to niche marketing, to truly fulfilling the promise of individualized marketing. What was formerly seen as a totally crazy idea—selling to a segment of one—is rapidly becoming the new marketing model.

The new marketing does not begin and end with mastering the bewildering array of automated tools driving today's Customer Relationship Management (CRM). Most companies don't get one-to-one marketing right because they remain primarily focused on the latest software technology rather than on the strategies and creative communications that create future value in interactive customer relationships.

Marching to this different drummer is dependent on playing a different tune—a new willingness to truly care about the customer in daring new ways. This "caring and daring" mind-set must be drilled down to the very core of the enterprise.

Who will be the first in each business category to create a corporate culture dedicated to exceeding what customers expect and winning their trust? These "marketing machines" of the future will become the new standard of excellence as buyers flock to their banner and keep coming back for more.

Whatever business you are in—whether selling to the consumer or to other businesses, whether an e-company entrepreneurial venture or an old-economy behemoth, whether selling a product or a service or an ingenious combination of both—putting the new marketing imperatives to work in your business can pay off big in the months and years ahead.

How far have we come in this exhilarating and perplexing journey into doing business in a Digital Age? The answer lies in how the personalized MaxiMarketing concepts of the 1980s have evolved into a new paradigm— the Max-e-Marketing of the Net Future.

Max-e-Marketing is the high road to maximizing profits with breakthrough info-tech applications that drive appropriate and effective interactive communication with targeted prospects and customers at all touch points online and offline.

Max-e-Marketing is about the creative strategies, communications, and interactions that add value for the customer while adding value to a company's bottom line. It's all about:

1. *Relationships*: How a business and all its employees interact with a prospect or a customer when it comes in contact with that person online or in any other communication channel. The common thread is to obtain a measurable response that updates the corporate knowledge base and leads to more responsive and productive future interactions.

2. *Experiences*: How each experience that a customer has with a company's products and services impacts the relationship. Delivering a pleasing experience involves the entire enterprise—end-to-end—as marketing becomes as much about process and operations as it is about creating a memorable advertising campaign or effective direct mail offer.

3. *Future value*: How you measure the value of the overall relationship with the company's customers and identify the drivers that impact the future value of that relationship. Measuring the return on investment (ROI) of an individual marketing campaign now takes second place to measuring the ROR (return on relationship), the return on the investment in building an enduring relationship with the company's customers, business partners, and stakeholders. The right relationships determine the future value of the business.

Marketing in this environment will be like nothing experienced in the last century. Creating a smiling customer now becomes the business of everyone from the call center representative, to the process engineers developing a new delivery system, to the truck driver delivering the product, to the newly crowned customer relationship manager and the CEO. Everyone who even remotely "touches" the customer will have to become a marketer in the true sense of the word—whether that person operates in virtual cyberspace or the bricks-and-mortar world.

In tracking the experiences of dozens of companies, the authors found some companies making the transition to the new personalized marketing with immediately gratifying results. But they also found many companies who only give lip service to this new way of thinking and resist allocating the budget dollars needed to implement it well. And there are far too many companies standing aside, running the risk of being left behind as they ponder which way to turn in the suddenly unfamiliar business landscape of the Net economy.

There is much to be learned from the innovative Internet entrepreneurs upsetting the practices of whole industries, from the old-economy companies making a U-turn in their strategic outlook, from the Michael Dells of the world who got it right more than a decade ago with the "be direct" business model.

Max-e-Marketing in the Net Future looks at where we are and spells out the new imperatives for coming out on top today. Taken together, these signposts can be a company's guide to what is needed to think differently and be a leader in the next wave of marketing innovation.

THE 7 MAX-E-MARKETING IMPERATIVES

1. Use What You Know to Drive What You Do—Make Everything You Do Add to What You Know

One of your most significant business assets is the demographic and behavioral information gained through direct interaction with customers online and offline. What you know, how you are organized to use it, and how you plan to add more of what you need to know can make the difference between success and failure in a networked economy driven by access to the right information.

2. Erase the Line Between Product and Service— Blend Services with Products to Create Offerings

No longer is it enough to simply market a product or a service. In the Net Future you will create tightly linked "offerings" without any separation. This fusion of products and services into a preemptive offering will differentiate your selling idea in a commoditized marketplace.

3. Make Each Relationship as Different as Each Customer—Add Relationship Equity to Brand Equity

In the Net Future, the convergence of customer knowledge and customer interaction produces a special experience for each individual at each touch point. The integration of sales, service, and customer care applications from the e-business world with traditional Customer Relationship Management processes can make each customer relationship as different as each person's data profile.

4. Do as Little as Possible Yourself—Others in the Net Economy Can Do It Better

Getting others to do as much of the work as possible is a key to success in the Net Future. Business partners, suppliers, distributors, and the end users are increasingly enlisted to do much of the "heavy lifting." This leaves your company free to focus on its core competence. Ask who is best suited to deliver each piece of the value proposition and be prepared to find that usually someone else can get it done faster and better than you can.

5. Make Your Interactive Process Become the Product—Now Is the Time for: The Process Is the Message

Two generations ago, Marshall McLuhan proclaimed: "The medium is the massage." Marketing's growing dependence on newly arrived TV at that time required a total rethinking of how to build a product brand. Now marketing's new dependence on e-system architecture and customer care software requires a rethink of what is most important in your selling proposition.

6. Factor Future Value into Every Move—Make the Brand Experience Exceed the Brand Perception

As direct interaction with the end user increasingly becomes the prevailing way of doing business, today's brand experience more and more will determine tomorrow's business ranking. What you do *to*, *for*, and *with* the customer that exceeds the brand perception builds brand equity and the future value of the relationship.

7. Make Business Responsible for Marketing and Marketing Responsible for Business—Form a New Partnership Between IT and Marketing

Now is the time to get everything *inside* your company lined up to serve customers *outside* your company. It is time to look at the changing role of marketing in a world of info-tech marvels and figure out how to move fast enough to keep up with escalating customer demands. It is time to form a new partnership between IT and marketing.

Each of the seven imperatives is presented in detail in the following chapters of *Max-e-Marketing in the Net Future*. The Net Future is arriving, and it's making itself felt 1 day at a time. As the cost of accessing data drops and the ease of accumulating data increases, the ability to build a meaningful dialogue with prospects and customers will continue to grow. The rising tide of technological change can only add to the usefulness of the Max-e-Marketing Imperatives in setting the right strategic direction.

THE BRAND RELATIONSHIP ERA

We are living through the shift from selling the same thing to as many people as possible a generation ago to fulfilling the individual needs and tastes of better informed consumers and business customers today. The battle against commoditization that shrinks profit margins is carried out with customized products, services, and offerings that increase profit margins.

It's a shift from "make a sale *now* at any cost" to building and managing relational databases that look at the lifetime value of each customer. It's a shift from reliance on a brand perception that often does not match up with the experience of the product or service to building brand equity by bonding with the customer.

This is a major change, from the "Sell! Sell! Sell!" era to the "Relationship is King" era. In the Net economy, it's the relationship that matters, not the selling. Each experience a person has with the brand rubs off on the brand relationship.

So just what is this brand relationship?

The *brand relationship* is the point at which brand perception and brand experience meet. In the Net Future, it is a primary factor in building brand equity.

It used to be that the perception fueled the experience. Now, with greater and greater frequency, it's the relationship experience that will cause the perception. As an extreme example, the recall on two continents of millions of Firestone tires mounted on Ford Explorers made a serious dent in the positive effect of hundreds of millions of dollars in advertising aimed at selling the perception of Ford as caring about the safety of its car buyers. Internet chat room buzz magnifies any misstep as never before.

THE EVOLUTION OF THE NEW MARKETING

The hype in the business press hailing the advent of an "e-business revolution" is unrelenting. Here is how BUSINESSWEEK ONLINE put it:

> The power to navigate the world at the click of a mouse is a force that is transforming our lives. The e-business revolution is upon us. And little will stay the same.[1]

However, the new marketing of the Net economy is about *evolution*, not revolution. According to Michael Dell, the CEO of Dell Computer: "Internet commerce is merely the direct-sales model on steroids."

The failure of the first wave of e-commerce entrepreneurs to realize that they were direct marketers in new clothing proved disastrous. By plowing 50, 60, and 70 percent of revenues into mostly silly brand-building advertising, rather than focusing on cost-effective direct response promotion to build Web traffic, they invented a totally out-of-sync business model.

To paraphrase the 1992 Democratic election campaign theme, the sign these neophyte e-tailers needed posted on the CEO's office wall was: "It's Direct Marketing, stupid."

The Darwinian progression of the new marketing from its direct marketing roots in the 1970s is easy to follow.

1970s—DIRECT MARKETING

It's the classic mode of selling without a middle person. Catalogs, direct–sales forces, subscription promotions, book clubs, and record clubs were the bulk of what made up this relatively small (10–15 percent of retail sales) but profitable corner of the U.S. economy. Back in those days, David Ogilvy frequently expressed his admiration for the accountability of direct response advertising. But almost nobody was listening.

1980s—INTEGRATED RELATIONSHIP MARKETING

A new variation that said any company can have a direct relationship with its customers—not just the direct marketers. *MaxiMarketing*, published in 1986, talked about one-to-one marketing—how information technology made it possible to address prospects and customers by name and known behavior characteristics and to build ever more sophisticated relational marketing databases.

The call went out to integrate the power of targeted "below-the-line" direct mail and telemarketing campaigns with the "above-the-line" commissionable marketing activities. It would not be until late in the next decade that the pejorative use of the terms "above" and "below" would fade away.

1990s—CUSTOMER RELATIONSHIP MANAGEMENT (CRM)

Arthur Andersen, McKinsey, PricewaterhouseCoopers, and management consulting companies worldwide began a love affair with CRM—the fashionable new life form of "going direct." In its new emergence as CRM, direct relationship marketing evolved into managing every aspect of increasing the value of the customer. The fact that it takes five to ten times more to acquire a new customer than it does to keep the one you have became common wisdom, and corporate top management awakened to the fact that customers were increasingly demanding world-class service.

2000s—MAX-E-MARKETING (DIRECT MASS MARKETING)

The rush to the Net took "direct" into the stratosphere. It made prospect and customer interaction affordable for any company, regardless of size or category. Now everyone can be a direct marketer with instant feedback from the marketplace. Amazon, AOL, and other pioneering Net leaders showed how to build a one-to-one relationship with tens of millions of customers. Buried deep in the genome of this new direct mass marketing was old-fashioned direct mail used by AOL to sign up new members by the millions. CRM soon was called e-CRM, with IT budgets shifting from a cost-reduction focus to projects focused on revenue generation and customer loyalty. And big bucks were poured into merging legacy databases with the flood of data coming from the Web connection.

CAPTURING THE HIGH GROUND IN THE NET FUTURE WITH THE FOUR A'S

Nothing in the Net Future changes the fact that a company still must identify its best prospects, convert them to customers, and deliver on the company's promises to them. And there are other fundamentals that remain.

Every brand manager who has ever set foot in a marketing course is familiar with the four P's of marketing:

- *Product*: What you're selling.
- *Price*: How much you're charging for the product or service.
- *Promotion*: How you're inducing people to buy it.
- *Place*: Where buyers can find it.

The four P's are still basic considerations, but in the Net economy the answers to those questions may be entirely different from what they have been in the past.

Now it is necessary to go beyond the four P's to focus on the four A's of direct mass marketing.

- *Addressability*: How do you identify and reach the best prospects and customers?
- *Accountability*: How easy is it to measure results?
- *Affordability*: How cost effective is it to interact with the customer?
- *Accessibility*: How can you locate the people you want to reach, and are they ready, willing, and able to receive your message?

Addressability and accountability were the hallmarks of the database marketing revolution of the 1980s. The rising commercialization of the Internet in the 1990s gave new life to both of those concepts and added whole new dimensions of affordability and accessibility to the interactive relationship marketing process.

While the four P's are product driven, the four A's are relationship driven. They focus on a holistic view of the customer, based on a continuous flow of fresh information—often reacted to in real time. To succeed in the twenty-first century, management will have to keep in mind the four A's as well as the four P's.

THE FULLY EVOLVED NEW MARKETING LIFE FORM

Internet technology offers a new dimension of addressability. Never before has it been so easy to target a marketing message so precisely and measure its results so quickly. The interactive nature of the medium provides opportunities for capturing not only traditional demographic information but data about online behavior, personal interests, and shifting priorities.

While carefully protecting and respecting the Web visitor's privacy, marketers can collect an astonishing amount of future targeting data. As use of the Net via wireless technology and personal digital assistants (PDAs) becomes increasingly widespread, it will become possible to control more precisely the timing of when a message is delivered. The recipient will receive the message only when he or she is most likely to act on it.

In the personalized, real-time environment of the Net, marketing campaigns can be modified to improve their chances of success while the campaign is actually going on. Rather than running focus groups or even analyzing early sales results in batches, both of which can be lengthy processes, companies can benefit from immediate measurement of whether a product or marketing message is actually turning into sales.

Once a company adopts the mind-set of a direct marketer, it can test its offers and everything else at the Web site on an unlimited scale at insignificant cost. Marketing literally becomes smarter by the moment.

REAL-TIME NABISCO B2B FEEDBACK

Now when it launches a sales campaign, Nabisco Food Service electronically sends marketing materials, including goals and objectives, to its sales team. It then gets real-time feedback from the field about the response from customers such as McDonald's.[2] This allows the marketing department to modify materials in an instant before other customers have seen them. As the campaign progresses, salespeople electronically rate the ease of execution, quality of sales materials based on customer feedback, and, ultimately, the overall effectiveness of the campaign itself.

This leads not only to improving the overall message but also to specific data about specific customers, which can ultimately make it easier to create customized marketing messages.

This has enormous implications for how a marketer conducts the rollout campaign. However, it becomes even more important that early participants be a good cross-section of the target market. If they are not, the entire campaign could be inappropriately skewed. In the case of Nabisco, it also involved changing the flow of information from only company to customer to include the flow from customer to company, as is discussed in greater detail in Imperative 1.

NET FUTURE MARKETING VS. TRADITIONAL MARKETING

Before turning to the presentation of each of the Max-e-Marketing Imperatives in the next seven chapters, Table I.1 shows how radically different the Max-e-Marketing approach is from what went before.

Individualized Max-e-Marketing is not solely about information flowing from the business to the customer or even about information flowing back from marketing campaigns aimed at the customer. It must be about information flowing from the customer to all parts of the organization.

No matter when, how, or where a customer contact occurs, information obtained as a result of that contact can help provide a three-dimensional picture in the company's database of that customer's interests, status, and likely future buying behavior.

Table 1.1 Differences Between Traditional Marketing and the Max-e-Marketing Way of Doing It

Traditional Marketing	Max-e-Marketing
Product driven	Relationship driven
Bombards the consumer with messages	Maintains dialogue with the consumer
Captures sales	Captures sales and data
Information flow is primarily one way	Information flow is two way
Responsibility of marketing department	Responsibility of entire company
Mass marketing model	Direct mass marketing
Closely held planning	Partners welcomed
New-technology resistant	New-technology friendly
Unknown prospects and customers	Addressable prospects and customers
Single-channel distribution	Multichannel distribution
Indirect, imprecise accountability	Real-time accountability

The problem is that developing a database is by itself not the solution to anything. A database is only a means to an end. The end is direct contact, dialogue, and brand-centric interaction with the prospect or customer that leads to a long-term, profitable relationship.

The good news is that it becomes much easier and much more affordable to make it happen when you begin to apply the 7 Max-e-Marketing Imperatives, as you will see demonstrated in the following chapters.

NOTES

1. BUSINESSWEEK ONLINE, March 22, 1999.
2. Based on the authors' interviews with several Nabisco senior executives.

Use What You Know to Drive What You Do

Make Everything You Do Add to What You Know

The chief information officer of a large financial institution once told us his bank had stored enough data on its customers that a printout would reach from the earth to the moon and back. What is being done with all that data? The bank hasn't yet decided.

A lot of companies are in the same position. Even though customer data is the currency of the Net Future, in many cases marketing managers simply have not yet come to terms with what to do with all the information that's being collected and stored.

Some are struggling with technology problems. Some have underestimated the amount of change required in their business processes to take advantage of the data. Some may use the data for ill-conceived promotions that focus only on short-term sales goals at the expense of building long-term customer relationships.

Other businesses are still just trying to capture the basic information needed to compete in the Net economy.

The Internet, with its interactive capabilities, ubiquitous access, and low cost of communication, has become an explosive new source of vital customer information gathered in real time. And, what we learn online can be tied to the legacy of offline knowledge stored in the company's computers. In the Net Future there will be an abundance of software that reads, understands, and makes sense of this mountain of information so that you can:

- Communicate with customers, based on their known preferences and needs.

- Offer relevant products and services based on known data, using the most cost-effective channels.

- Reap the rewards of direct contact with consumers to influence their buying behavior, based on their individual criteria.

In this new world of interactive communication, the goal is to make every marketing decision and action accountable in building and sustaining the most profitable customer relationships.

In short, it's about Max-e-Marketing.

Max-e-Marketers maximize sales and profits by means of appropriate and effective interaction with known prospects and customers across all touch points online and offline.

Taking advantage of the ease and low cost of interaction on the Internet means learning new ways to constantly get more information to improve the customer experience. Companies that act now to collect, analyze, and use this knowledge will be able to profit in ways that were unimaginable only a few years ago.

When you make everything you do add to what you know, you can take full advantage of the possibilities for establishing truly responsive relationships with each customer—relationships that are driven by what is known about that individual's preferences, interests, and past behavior.

TAKING STOCK OF YOUR INFORMATION ASSETS

In many cases, valuable information already exists within the company, but because that information isn't organized in a meaningful way, it cannot be used effectively.

The first step to becoming a relationship-driven marketer is to assess your current customer information assets.

WHAT IS THE RIGHT DATA?

Before you start using what you know to drive what you do, you want to know what you need to know. Sounds obvious. But it is the first place a would-be Max-e-Marketer is likely to do less than what is indicated. It requires undertaking a strategic planning process that managers often may bypass because it is difficult. It requires cooperation across multiple departments that may be accustomed to full autonomy and don't see the broader relationship opportunities. But this process is a crucial starting point, because it lays the foundation for everyone in the company to recognize the enterprise value of customer data.

A key consideration in this evaluation is to determine the kinds of information that can help you create and retain the most profitable and long-lasting relationships possible. Many companies have rushed to market with surveys, promotions, or registration forms intended to gather lots of customer data, only to find later that they had forgotten to ask for key data elements.

For example, one dot-com company realized too late that its promotional contests, designed to acquire new customers, were attracting a high proportion of minors who would be unable to afford its products.

HOW MUCH OF THIS USEFUL DATA DO YOU ALREADY HAVE?

Exactly how much do you know about your customers today? Beyond name, address, and perhaps phone number, how many actual data points do you have on each customer? How many fit the criteria you established as being needed to drive profitable business relationships? A company may find that it already has a good deal of the data it needs, but it isn't easily accessible. Now, in the Net economy, resources are available to sort through huge data banks to assess the value and significance of information. You can prioritize what you know with an effectiveness never before possible. You can create systems to link old and new information, as well as to add new data with every customer and prospect contact.

WHAT DATA IS MISSING?

Many in-house customer databases have been growing for years, sometimes taking on lives of their own. The bad news: the data they contain may not match your needs in the Net Future. Your audit must identify what types of data are missing and create a plan for obtaining the information.

Missing data can often be obtained by changing data-collection practices. What exists may also be enhanced with data that is available from public sources, commercial databases, or data-sharing agreements with marketing partners.

For example, a company that realizes it is failing to identify how many of its online shoppers are repeat visitors can easily change its own data collection and monitoring practices. A company that wants to reach new prospects or offer new value to existing customers may partner with another company to create a custom publication or outsource its loyalty program. If a company wants to create a predictive model to target its next promotion toward prospects most likely to respond and buy, it may need to overlay its file with additional demographic elements such as age, income, or home ownership. In many countries, new processing technologies are making it easier to enhance data files—for a fee—from numerous sources.

HOW ACCESSIBLE IS THE DATA?

The larger the company, the greater the chance that valuable information is locked up in multiple databases that were built over time by different divisions to support very different purposes. Extracting and linking up the data to get a cross-enterprise view of the customer base can be a costly and technically difficult project.

What's more, each profit center in the company usually wants to "own" the data, to better serve its specific customer sets. Cross-company linkage often requires a strong, high-level champion to get cooperation from the current "owners" of the data. But without making all the data accessible to everyone in the company who can use it, it will not be possible to maximize sales and profits.

WHO DOES WHAT WITH THE DATA NOW?

Finding out who within an organization is collecting and using customer data is a crucial process that can yield surprising insights about how many relationships a customer already has with a company. A publishing operation, for example, may collect basic mailing information about subscribers in the Circulation Department. But the Advertising Department is likely to augment it for use in creating personalized advertising campaigns for ad clients. And any new interactive publishing efforts would be collecting valuable online user data from online subscribers.

Other industries likewise may have predictable patterns for where data is collected and used within an organization.

- Manufacturers may have numerous product divisions collecting information about customers without realizing that the same customer does business across product lines or in both his or her professional and personal lives.

- Financial institutions have been pacesetters in focusing on cross-product consumer behaviors and assessing how to act like one company with customers who have money invested across multiple distribution channels.

- The professional divisions of pharmaceutical companies maintain massive databases about doctors and health care institutions, and are increasingly building databases of consumers who respond to mass market campaigns by requesting literature about products or illnesses.

Within every industry and company, identifiable patterns of data usage can help determine how customer and market information can be managed and used effectively.

WHAT PUBLICLY AVAILABLE DATA SOURCES CAN BE USED?

Depending on geography, you may be able to supplement your own databases by buying or renting those of others. However, there are enormous differences in what is available in various parts of the world. The ability to use other sources may be affected by privacy legislation and how advanced data collection is in a given area.

In the European community, a regional directive imposes strict limitations on the use of data about customer shopping behaviors. It generally requires that a marketer, who must obtain permission for that use, tell consumers explicitly about intended use of their information. In South America, reliable, legal sources of data are very hard to find. In the Far East and much of the South Pacific, data markets are still very immature, and regulators there are looking to Europe for direction.

However, as the Internet takes a more central role in shaping the e-business of the Net Future on every continent, markets around the world will likely move closer to the North American model.

The United States currently has the most open data markets in the world, and a wide array of compiled data-bases and response files can be rented for various uses. If a company needs to augment existing data elements, overlays can be purchased in the United States from sources such as Acxiom, Experion, and others.

Acxiom now offers an advanced Net Future capability to link all known occurrences of an individual customer across a company's many systems. Whether Rose Dugas shows up in a monthly billing system or an up-to-the-moment e-commerce transaction, Acxiom's new linking technology, AbiliTec, can help a company identify her as the same indi-vidual. This can shortcut many months of programming and development work to get a holistic view of customer relationships across the enterprise.

AbiliTec, combined with new application integration technologies, enables the marketer to instantly recognize a customer at any touch point. This improves the speed and quality of the interaction, ensuring its relevance to the customer. If the customer just went online 10 minutes ago, and is now calling the customer care center, his or her latest actions at the Web site are known and available to the representative handling that call.

HOW IS THE DATA ORGANIZED?

Creating the infrastructure for extracting data from existing systems, assembling it, and augmenting it with new transac-tion data from online and other sources will be a continuing challenge. It's one reason why customer data-integration technologies are such a priority for most IT managers.

IT'S ALL ABOUT INFORMATION

THINK SCALABLE

Imagine what kind of information you'd like to have and how you'd like to use it. You probably won't be able to do it all—and you almost certainly won't get it all at one time—but thinking big can help prevent developing a system that's inadequate by the time it's launched. And with ever-increasing amounts of data being processed online and offline, this is no time to underestimate demand.

THINK MODULAR

The more modular the information, the more flexibility there is in how it's used.

THINK CURRENT

An outdated database is worse than no database at all. In the ever-changing world of the Internet, real-time data will increasingly become the engine that drives decision making. Periodic batch updates are no longer enough for marketers who need to know what a customer did a minute ago on the company's Web site.

THINK ACCESSIBLE

Levels of access to information are a key component of info-tech strategy. You'll not only have to balance the need for customer access to information with the need for security, but also to think about how to distribute information throughout your company and its extended network of business partners and suppliers. The Internet is bringing into question many of the same issues that arose when PCs began to invade the corporate world. IT departments panicked at the thought of throwing open the gates to the company's information banks. Linking to business partners is raising similar issues now. When in doubt, go for making information more available instead of less and leverage that accessibility to the hilt.

Establishing reliable operations that can accommodate data from disparate systems, mine the data, and manage marketing campaigns and customer relationships has never been more important. It is essential that marketing and IT professionals work together to ensure that the infrastructure supports the organization's strategic goals.

THE DATABASE IS THE MARKETPLACE AT MEREDITH

As publisher of books, special-interest publications, and magazines such as *Ladies' Home Journal* and *Better Homes and Gardens*, Meredith Corporation is perhaps best known as a U.S. media giant. But in the last decade, its use of data-driven marketing has made its rich databases as important to its overall business success as its publications. Its use of the Internet is enabling the company to create added value for its advertisers and for the readers of its publications.

The Des Moines–based company, founded in 1902, employs almost 3000 people. It has 20-plus magazine properties, 12 television stations that reach almost 10 percent of all U.S. TV households, and has published 300 books and more than 100 special-interest publications on subjects such as cooking and building.

What is not commonly known about Meredith is that it has evolved into a database marketing company that prides itself on its use of consumer data and leverages each nugget of information it collects to help its customers (the advertisers in its publications) better serve their customers (consumers).[1]

When the company transformation started more than 10 years ago, established industry practice was to maintain separate circulation and advertising databanks for each publication. Advertisers had little more than broad-based information about the readers of those publications beyond syndicated research about the general population.

Meredith decided to invest in integrating these individual market-oriented databases. The company now has information on about 7 out of every 10 home-owning households in the United States. On each consumer, it maintains about 300 individual data points.

"We wanted to put the databases together to provide consumer information to our advertising customers. That was the biggest thing we did 10 years ago," says Steve Lacy, President of Meredith's Integrated and Interactive Media Group. "We wanted to target direct marketing activities across all the properties. This was our plan to support our direct mail activities. Also, companies such as Procter & Gamble and Kraft wanted to better target through our magazines. The information we have about the consumer helps them create the right products."

SERVING A CUSTOMER'S CUSTOMER

Every marketing effort, whether for its own circulation base or for an advertiser's direct-response marketing campaign, is carefully tracked and added to the company's integrated knowledge base.

"The knowledge is a tremendous asset," says Lacy. "We figured out in an opportunistic way how to service our direct mail. As it evolved, and we established integrated marketing, we found we could help our customers communicate better and more directly with their customers."

For example, Meredith found that there was a correlation between gardening and minivan owners. "We worked with Chrysler and found this out by overlaying lists of consumers." Meredith then worked with the automotive industry to provide gardening books and publications as incentives for consumers to visit specific minivan dealers, helping its customers reach the right prospects in the right way. "We're pretty sure we have the most well-defined consumer database of any of our competitors."

The Internet has provided Meredith with a rocket-booster for its data-collection engine. It has not only allowed the company to leverage what it knows about subscribers but also has provided a cost-effective way to continue to add to that data source.

"We're trying very hard to make the database evolve because with the interactive environment we can get a whole lot more information," says Lacy.

Over time, Meredith has developed three methods to accumulate and fine-tune useful information:

1. *The drip technique*: This is the direct, consumer-contact model. Whenever a consumer contacts Meredith, whether by telephone, mail, or through any of its Web sites, the company gently probes for a bit more information about that person. "We add to the information we have in small chunks. We ask just a little more each time we talk to you," says Lacy. All that information is funneled into consolidated central databases.

2. *Mapping*: The Net gives Meredith the ability to see where its visitors go. "We keep track of the activity whether you're in the 'home improvement' or the 'recipe' database. We can track back to the user ID. We also do a lot of focus groups and a lot of testing."

3. *Overlays*: These provide more descriptive information about types of users and their preferences. Meredith is a big believer in lists: customer lists, lists from the government, lists from competitors, or any list that helps the company determine how certain types of people behave in certain ways. Each list adds to the storehouse of information that increases its targeting capability.

"Why does a supermarket stack Tide to the ceiling and leave it that way for every customer? How is the consumer who shops on Thursday different from the one who shops on Sunday morning, and how are those consumer needs different from each other? Companies are too focused on products and not enough on customers," says Lacy. He goes on to say, "The best way to get a customer is to serve them a product they're interested in. What we know about the consumer lets us drive our business. Some other companies are still run as silos, as individual businesses. . . .The more you communicate with us, the more data points we have."

For most companies, Lacy recommends a four-step process to become customer data-centric:

1. Buy as many lists as you can to add relevant overlay data.
2. Do a lot of data-driven direct mail testing.
3. Capture as much information as you can on the Web.
4. Buy "the right technology " and use it to integrate what you learn from diverse sources.

The technology is needed to de-duplicate information and mine the data to find correlations among various profiles and behaviors. Lacy comments:

"There are all sorts of companies that operate as silos when they communicate with a consumer. They need to have a consolidated view of the consumer.

"The traditional mode is to sell products. What you want to do is see how you solve a consumer's problem and deal with it from that direction. The more levels between the manufacturer and the consumer, the more difficult it is. Most retailers don't know a great deal about their customers."

Meredith keeps all its data in one data center, where it focuses a large amount of its effort in keeping that information up to date. While one group of people is responsible for accumulating and updating the data, another group functions as internal and external consultants to the business units. "They help the customers figure out the best way to mine the data out of the database," says Lacy.

Meredith figured out over time that just building a database does not a business make. It takes building, fine-tuning, updating, centralizing, cleaning, and continual refreshing. Every customer contact adds value to Meredith's database, and the company is often approached by other companies to take over their database operations.

At this pacesetting Max-e-Marketer, there is a fierce concentration on using what is known about the consumer to drive what they do for the advertiser, and everything Meredith does adds to what they know about end users.

"We basically gather and retain information about what a consumer does, which gives us knowledge of how to speak to the consumer. This is now part of our culture."

TURNING THE FIREHOSE OF INFORMATION ON YOURSELF AT NABISCO FOOD SERVICE

Nabisco generally brings to mind images of cookies. After all, who hasn't spent at least part of his or her childhood either munching on Fig Newtons or twisting off the chocolate ends of an Oreo to lick off the cream filling on the inside?

But there is another side to Nabisco. It also has a business-to-business division called Nabisco Food Service. Every time you sit down in a restaurant or eat at a fast-food facility, you're likely to use a Nabisco product. Besides

Oreos and Fig Newtons, Nabisco boasts such brands as A1 Steak Sauce, Grey Poupon mustard, Ritz crackers, Life Savers, and Planters peanuts.

Nabisco Food Service sells about $400 million worth of those products to restaurants each year, going through major distributors, such as Sysco. What is different at Nabisco as it adjusts to the Net economy is that the seller-to-buyer information flow is being reversed.

Knowing how to collect and use that information is a key strategic competitive weapon, says Steven Rudnitsky, President of Nabisco Food Service:[2]

"In food service, the industry is evolving as we speak," says Rudnitsky. Manufacturers and distributors all have various designs in terms of how they market to the 500,000 restaurants around the country. "Historically, a sales-person would go in and see each individual customer and sell all the products they had in their book. Now all the information is available electronically so the distributor has a fully automated book. And the value of the distributor changes."

It is this change in who has the information and when that turns many business propositions on their heads. In the past, the producer had all the power. It not only controlled the products but it also decided what products were created, how they were marketed, and the actual information flow to the buyer.

In the Net economy, the buyer has most of the power, as Nabisco Food Service realizes. "If chefs want to make something, they can now go into a distributor's database and see the menu and all the options," says Rudnitsky. "They can see what they need and order it. It's not only the recipe management and value of the product available online that's giving any chef the opportunity to create something new. It's the experience of doing that that is so different from in the past."

In this and many similar situations and in companies in many different categories, the change in information flow changes the actual business.

"The chef is the buyer, but the distributor is not the same seller of yesteryear," says Rudnitsky.

"It's like Amazon's ability to create new options that is vastly different than the way things were in the past. The buyer is doing the buying and the seller isn't doing the selling. The information takes on a whole new value.

"When a buyer is buying, the information available today gives them exponential opportunity. As a result, the seller needs to respond to that opportunity."

Nabisco realized that to succeed in this environment, it had to rethink its product mix and how it interacted with its customers. Rudnitsky says:

"It's the information itself that creates a new model. It becomes crucial to create value-added products, via services, for the buyer. The cycle then is complete, because as the buyer is ordering, real-time information is being fed back to the distributor."

With this recognition of change in information flow, Nabisco changed how it operates with its own internal information flow and created a real-time feedback process for its sales staff.

When presenting their marketing materials and sales pitch to a restaurant, rather than simply taking the order (or not), the salesperson now captures feedback from the customer placing the order.

That feedback is instantly transmitted via pre-created formats on each salesperson's laptop computer, enabling the marketing department to instantly monitor a campaign's degree of success. In addition, the sales staff rates various features of the campaign, such as ease of execution and quality of materials.

Nabisco uses its sales staff to make everything it does add to Nabisco's marketing knowledge bank. What is added to what Nabisco already knows, in true Max-e-Marketing fashion, is translated into real-time feedback that can impact the bottom line.

"The role of the seller in the past has been to ensure that the products they marketed are available when needed," says Rudnitsky. "In the future, the seller could become the tracker of the buyer's information needs, as the information flow totally changes from the company, to the seller, to the buyer."

That information flow, in turn, will determine which products Nabisco Food Service needs to manufacture and in what quantities.

THE 51 PERCENT RULE

The experience of Nabisco Food Service demonstrates a key difference between traditional marketing and Net Future thinking. The direction of the flow of information in most organizations needs to change (see Table 1.1).

Traditional marketing has focused on getting information to the customer. Even when market research became the foundation of marketing strategy, it had a mass focus rather than an individual focus. The goal was to help understand consumer behavior in the aggregate to forecast general reaction to specific products prior to introduction.

Companies traditionally have been organized and grown through the creation, manufacture, and distribution of new products. This is one reason why product managers within a company filled with well-known brands are held in such high regard internally (not to mention the political power they have within the organization).

The product brings the revenue, so more focus is on the product. Better products result in more revenue. More sales of a given product often increase profit margins, as production efficiencies increase. Much of the customer contact is handled through resellers.

With the new marketing, the emphasis shifts to gaining as much information about customers as possible. And we focus on the mix of information then directed at each individual through traditional channels and online.

In the *Digital Estate*, Chuck Martin said that to be truly connected to its customers, a company should keep internal e-mail below 50 percent and external e-mail over 50 percent.[3] In the interconnected world of the Net Future, this approach extends beyond e-mail.

The 51 percent rule of Max-e-Marketing says that at least 51 percent of all communications—from the Net, e-mail, phone, or postal mail—should originate from external sources and be circulated throughout the organization. This refers to information that can help everyone understand the external marketing environment and what customers want.

This has important implications for how a company needs to think about each customer interaction. Among other things, companies that have traditionally been connected only through resellers are beginning to find tremendous value in making a more direct connection with the ultimate customer, even though the traditional resellers may remain in place.

Table 1.1 Implementing the 51 Percent Rule

Traditional customer-information sources	Net economy customer information sources
Market research (focus groups, paid syndicated research)	Real-time customer inquiries Geographic positioning systems
Customer feedback (letters, suggestion boxes, customer service)	Online chat rooms and bulletin boards Tracking of customer behavior on the Web
Sales force anecdotes	Quantitative data based on real-time analysis of sales transactions
Data mining of batched information about customer transactions	Data mining of contact information—transactions and inquiries—in real time
Mailing lists organized by demographics	Permission-based e-mail

Pharmaceutical companies, for example, have awakened to the advantage of augmenting indirect channels of contact with more direct methods. Health care remains one of the top categories of information researched via the Web.

The drug makers have begun offering helpful information via the Web as a way to build brand recognition and capture new customer information. This has changed the marketing dynamic for nearly all drug companies, which want to alert patients—potential customers—to breakthrough treatments and get those patients to see their brands associated with particular ailments, treatments, and/or cures.

Pharmaceutical companies now have entire marketing divisions devoted to nothing but developing resources to reach Web-enlightened prospects.

USING KNOWLEDGE THROUGHOUT THE BUYING CYCLE

In the Net economy, the buying process itself doesn't change. Predictably, it involves a logical progression:

Suspect → Prospect → Customer → Advocate → Partner

The process also involves activity phases that often lead to such conversion:

Brand awareness → Passive interest → Active shopping → Purchase

Maximizing customer value and creating true advocates and even partners requires:

Customer development → Customer retention → Reshopping → Repurchase

With vastly increased customer information stored in relational databases, Max-e-Marketers are in an unprecedented position to understand and make the most of buying cycles. Your brand can now be in exactly the right place (top of mind) when a suspect or prospect is identified as having passive interest and be nudged to active shopping.

Max-e-Marketing also allows you to target prospects moving in and out of buying phases. It becomes much easier to find people whom you want to reach when scores of syndicators are gathering and making available updated information about personal interests and desires every day on the Web.

You also now have the potential of moving some buying decisions from one part of the buying cycle to another.

MOVING FROM EVENT-TRIGGERED CYCLE TO TIME-LAPSE CYCLE

- Replacing a fan belt is often an event-triggered buying decision; it tends to happen after someone has been left by the side of the road with an over-heated engine. However, automobile manufacturers are developing cars that will automatically run diagnostic checks to determine when certain parts are on the verge of needing to be replaced. An event-triggered cycle becomes a time-lapse cycle triggered when the clock says it's time for a change.

- Appliance makers are working on giving consumers the ability to detect when supplies are about to run low. A scanner run over the bar code on an emptying jar of jam and a message from a disposable chip embedded in a milk carton can notify a grocery-delivery company to bring more jam or milk on the next scheduled delivery.

MOVING FROM TIME-LAPSE CYCLE TO EVENT-TRIGGERED CYCLE

- Shoe manufacturers recommend replacing running shoes every 6 months. However, a manufacturer that has a good customer-information database could convert its time-lapse cycle to one triggered by an event of the company's own making.

    The shoe manufacturer could track customers who are nearing the 6-month repeat purchase and contact them with an offer designed to shorten that time frame. The company might offer a discount to customers who are willing to make their purchases at a time when the company has a backlog of inventory it needs to move. A direct relationship with the customer can accelerate the purchase time lapse.

- The same strategy could be used for magazine subscriptions and the automotive industry, which typically generate time-lapse purchases.

Other types of transactions also can be shifted from a time-lapse cycle to an event-triggered cycle. In the near future, vending machines will have the ability to electronically notify the supplier exactly when they need replenishment. Trucks that now make regular rounds with huge inventories can schedule routes and inventories, based on actual, event-triggered demand.

EACH MAX-E-MARKETING IMPERATIVE SETS THE STAGE FOR THE NEXT IMPERATIVE

The new technologies that allow information to flow freely in every direction, largely independent of artificial obstacles, are a fundamental platform underpinning the Net economy. They enable creative business management to find exciting new ways to use what is known about the customer.

One of the most valuable side effects of making everything you do add to what you know is the knowledge it provides about how to blend services with products to create offerings—the focus of the Max-e-Marketing imperative discussed next.

NOTES

1. The following is based on the authors' interviews with Steve Lacy, Meredith's President of Integrated and Interactive Media Group.
2. The following is based on the authors' interview with Steven Rudnitsky, President of Nabisco Food Service.
3. From Chuck Martin, *The Top 10 Rules of Business Netiquette in the Digital Estate*, New York: McGraw-Hill, 1997.

Erase the Line Between Product and Service

Blend Services with Products to Create Offerings

Knowing as much as possible about customers is a critical first step. However, customer knowledge is meaningless unless it is leveraged to generate value. And one of the most important ways to do that is to use customer knowledge to help understand what should be created and produced for those customers.

No longer is it enough to simply market a product or a service alone. In the Net Future, products and services alone must be so tightly linked that it becomes impossible to see where intangible benefits end and tangible benefits begin. And that interconnection must not be limited to the selling process; it must drive the product development process from its inception to create what we call an "offering."

WHERE DO PRODUCTS FIT?

Companies historically were organized around the design of products, often to the point that entire divisions would focus on creating and marketing single categories of products. In many cases, companies would organize to sell these products to a designated market of buyers, usually with the big buyers receiving the most attention.

Matrix organizations, such as IBM, would organize sales forces around industries and line up the various product groups necessary to support that industry. The results were very tangible, as the amount of products sold to one company could be accounted for, with the advantage flowing to whomever got the price, promotion, and placement right.

But an Internet-driven world is less about tangible items than about intangibles. What flows over the Net is not "stuff" but information about the "stuff." As a result, staying product-focused alone is no longer enough to guarantee success.

The networked environment increasingly affects how the offering is created, sold, and distributed. The networking of everything creates a new dilemma for the makers of products. With instant access to all information all the time, buyers can instantly measure supply against demand, feature against feature, price against price, with the market itself determining the real value of a product at any given moment.

This can lead to an increasing commoditization of many products, at least in the short term, as sellers quickly respond to one another's fleeting advantage.

Additional factors leading to this increasing product commoditization include:

- *New and expanded competition*: The Net has facili-
  tated not only global commerce but also the emergence of many new companies. More competition
  leads to greater pressure on price.

- *The emergence of flex pricing*: Online auctions have
  meant that prices often are tied more to customer
  demand than to brand positioning or a product feature.
  Buyers are being conditioned to expect different prices
  for different items at different times, based on demand.

- *The emergence of digital, business-to-business
  marketplaces*: An e-marketplace puts competitors
  side by side, making differentiation more difficult.
  Since entire supply chains can be aggregated,
  dynamic comparison shopping can further impact
  product pricing.

- *Automated shopping agents*: These services scour
  the Net to present buyers with price comparisons
  from different sellers on identical items.

THE GREAT VALUE SHIFT

Adding to the leveling of prices for various products is
what see as "the great value shift." The e-business environment turns the value proposition for the creation, distribution, sale, and consumption of products on its head.
This new dynamic ultimately will affect not only pricing but
also determine the value of what is being sold.

In the great value shift of the networked environment,
core assets can actually become peripheral. A company
can find itself in a totally different business from that of the
past, as it discovers that its core assets are less profitable
or less well positioned for the future than what surrounds
and supplements the actual product.

Commoditization can affect just about any product, from hard to soft goods as the nature of the business environment changes.

This shift has already touched the value of real-time stock quotes, traditionally available only to brokers who were charged a stiff fee by the New York Stock Exchange. Real-time and slightly delayed quotes are now distributed free, when not long ago the standard fee for real-time quotes was $29.95 a month.

It has touched multiple listing service real estate listings, traditionally a valued asset for participating brokers. They're now available in abridged form at Cyberhomes.com in various cities while Owners.com allows buyers who want to sell their homes on their own to post a picture, property data, and price. Not to be left behind, The National Association of Realtors, through its Realtor.com Web site, provides potential buyers with centralized listings for most of the United States.

When products or services are commoditized, you must find other ways to provide added value—something that people will be willing to pay for. In many cases, what used to be a core asset can become a loss leader, with peripheral products and services creating an offering that drives new revenue streams. The concept behind the inexpensive six-pack of soda that gets a consumer into the store to buy $10 worth of groceries now can be applied to a wide variety of products and services.

- When Auto-by-Tel can get a buyer a car for a few hundred dollars over dealer cost, it shifts value from the auto dealer network to the service Auto-by-Tel provides.

- When an insurance company ultimately offers the car at cost if you agree to use that agency for insurance during the ownership period, the value shift moves up a notch. The value of the car to the insurance company is barely an issue; the value is in the insurance and the potentially new customer relationship.

• Increasingly, the value of the car you buy will be connected to the unique services in the offering. General Motors offers the OnStar system on a number of its vehicles. In an emergency the driver pushes a button and an OnStar advisor is instantly connected via phone directly to the vehicle. The OnStar system locates the exact position through GPS (global positioning system) technology. Need directions or a restaurant reservation? OnStar concierge services can handle that too. Or it can locate the nearest ATM, hospital, convenience store, gas station, and hotel—and book a hotel room. At least part of the value of the car now comes from those services.

Typically, the driver of a value shift will be from outside an industry. It can be a company that in the past hasn't been selling that particular product, as in the insurance company automotive example. The insurance company doesn't really care about the car, just about selling the insurance. Meanwhile, the affected car dealers are still looking at other local car dealers as their primary competition. Any industry that looks only at the traditional competitive landscape is vulnerable to value shifting from a completely unexpected source.

To the real estate agent, the central real estate listing is the traditional core asset. In the new marketing, realtors might give a local newspaper the rights to print and distribute the listings. The newspaper then could add context around the listing, such as information on local schools, demographics of the neighborhood, and distance to shopping centers. The enhanced offering adds value for the newspaper, the real estate agency, and the potential home buyer.

After the house is purchased, the real estate agency might offer the data on the individual to after-sale services such as moving companies, lawn services, and insurance brokers. The real estate listing itself becomes a commodity, with the value shifting to the surrounding transactions.

A prime example of value shifting is now taking place in the travel industry. Convenience in supplying travel arrangements was the core competency of travel agencies. However, airlines, Travelocity, Priceline, and others are the new competition with their search services and superdiscounted tickets on the Web. The airlines in this new world reduced commissions to agents. While Delta was going so far as to try charging a surcharge on tickets *not* purchased online, many travel agents were starting to charge travelers a fee for issuing airline tickets.

In some ways, the travel itself becomes the commodity, and agents face an array of new competitors and the prospect of finding other revenue streams for their services.

Marketers are offering new models for aggregating frequent-flier miles. Aggregation will change the business model so that the value is not necessarily in the ticket sale, but rather in selling loyalty rewards for companies that want to reach frequent flyers. The added value is in the offering that surrounds the ticket sale.

The challenge, and opportunity, of the great value shift is to shift value from someone else's product or service to what you are offering.

Part of the opportunity is also to see where the core product or service can be leveraged to provide an unrelated — and often unexpected—experience.

Many companies are beginning to realize this and are creating added value for the customer relationship in this way. Some examples are given in Table 2.1.

Table 2.1 Value Shift Examples

Company	Value Shift
John Deere	Provides health-planning services and an HMO for small businesses.
Wal-Mart	Sells real estate and plane tickets.
Sony	Hosts an online Jeopardy Game.
Burger King	Gives away Web access with a Whopper on terminals inside some restaurants.
CNN	Provides Web-based health care information.
GE	Offers education planning and mortgage services.
K-Mart	Gives away free Internet access.
Ford	Sells T-shirts, hats, and accessories to complement your new car.
Sears	Delivers flowers.
JC Penney	Sells pharmaceuticals.
Martha Stewart Living	Promotes branded products for K-Mart through branded magazine.
Disney	Sends recipes to your friends.
Safeway	Has a digital birthday card service.

THE OFFERING

One way a company can protect itself against a possible value shift in its business category is to do the value shifting itself. Marketers need to look for ways to expand what the company provides its customers. The Max-e-Marketing model for doing this is to create an offering.

An *offering* is a tight unification of product and service that better satisfies customer wants and needs, and helps enhance the future value of the customer relationship.

Converting to an offering approach allows companies to focus on deepening relationships with customers, while at the same time repositioning what they offer in the eyes of those customers.

EXPANDING THE PRODUCT AND SERVICE

In an offering, what is being sold is not simply a combination of product and service. It meshes the benefits of product and service so well that it creates something that is more than the sum of its parts. The ultimate example of this is Reflect.com, which is discussed in greater detail in Imperative 3. The company lets customers blend their own customized personal care products over the Net; the product (cosmetics) is inseparable from the way in which it is created by the customers themselves.

EXPANDING THE RELATIONSHIP

An offering takes into account not only what is being sold but also how it is being used. It looks at what other needs and interests a customer has and how the offering can be expanded to satisfy them.

EXPANDING THE FUTURE VALUE OF THE CUSTOMER EXPERIENCE

An offering addresses a customer's needs, wants, and interests. But it does so in a way that encourages customer loyalty and additional purchases. An offering focuses not only on what is being sold but also on how that purchase can be leveraged for upselling, cross-selling, and selling something entirely new to that person.

An offering includes not only product and service but also the customer's interaction with it.

To truly unlock future value, an offering must be structured in such a way that it maximizes the opportunities to gain valuable customer information. That information can, in turn, drive future sales and the development of new offerings. A company must take into account customer support as an integral part of the offering itself rather than as an added-value proposition or, worse, an afterthought.

The *offering* concept can have a profound effect on how a company thinks about what it is providing its customers.

Providing an offering is very different from selling a product or service. For one thing, it acknowledges that the customer is in the driver's seat. Pleasing the customer becomes paramount. *Selling* implies convincing the customer of the value of a product or service. Even the softer term *marketing* still places the product at the core of the process.

In the Net Future, the emphasis switches from a company selling to a buyer choosing. When you provide an offering, you recognize that the customer is in control of the process of deciding how to satisfy his or her real preferences.

COMPLEX PRODUCTS REQUIRE OFFERINGS

Technology vendors no longer sell products; they sell "solutions." Though some look at this transition as simply a marketing technique, it was borne out of necessity.

In many instances, technology and telecommunications products have become so complex and require so much training, maintenance, and upgrading that service and support become as important to the initial purchase as the product itself.

This is one of the reasons why established brands with reputation and track records of supporting customers have a short-term advantage. They have greater resources to draw on in supplying the peripheral service and support. However, the reliance on "solution selling" underscores the fact that the product itself is simply no longer enough.

SERVICES TAKE THE LEAD

An offering takes advantage of the Net's ability to provide intangibles at a low cost. Even though marrying products and services may initially cost more to provide, the offering can ultimately offer better profit margins.

Without inventory and manufacturing costs, the services component is potentially more profitable, especially if parts of the process can be automated.

Unique services can be price blind. When a service is new, nobody knows what the price should be. There's less risk of comparison shopping for price/value, so there is less pressure from commoditization.

In some cases, a higher value can be placed on an offering simply because it is provided first, ahead of competitors. This is part of the thinking of many Net startups that fiercely focused on being first to market.

Services can help to insulate a product from being leapfrogged by a competitor with snazzier technology or better product features. So intense is the rush to gain competitive advantage that a product's life cycle is shorter than ever before.

There is greater pressure than ever before to grab market share before a competitor can duplicate whatever it is a business is doing—and add a feature or improve a service to strengthen the offering. For example:

- In New York City, where life often takes on a frenetic pace, one company set up Internet architecture to facilitate users entering requests for delivery services (at home or at work) of anything wanted within 1 hour. Within months, an imitator one-upped that company with a specialty delivery program: door-to-door in 30 minutes. Guess which one has the advantage now—and the price premium as a result?

- Think about what happened with robotic lawn-mowers. When one company introduced a self-propelled mower activated and guided by tracking devices imbedded beneath the grass, a similar competing device was on the market from another company just months later.

- It was not Sony that made it to market first with DDS (digital data storage) technology, but Sony went head to head with its own version of the mass storage computer backup product in less than 6 months and achieved greater market share than the original device manufacturer. Sony's product launch could take a full-bore "our-product's-better-because" approach, since Sony could improve on what had been built before.

- *Wired* magazine showed how to embed microcuing devices for scanner or personal digital assistant (PDA) technologies into printed advertisements that directly and immediately link interested readers to the advertiser's Web site. Now *Forbes* magazine, *AdWeek,* and others also provide devices for reading ads and bringing readers automatically to appropriate Web sites. Similarly, in point-and-click fashion, you will soon be able to direct your PDA to AdAlive airport concourse billboards and connect to the Internet. You'll not only access the sponsor's site but you'll also have a free browser to search the Internet as well.

MORE CUSTOMER CONTACT

Doing business in a different way, services can help to create an ongoing bond with the customer that, once established, can be difficult to poach. That one-of-a-kind relationship can help combat commoditization. Buyers don't just go to Amazon because the online retailer sells a lot of products. They go because they have a satisfying and unique experience.

Another great benefit of the Max-e-Marketing imperative of erasing the line between product and service is that services provide ongoing opportunities for customer contact. This presents more opportunities for the kind of information-gathering and customer knowledge that can help build the relationship between you and the customer. Companies can leverage these interactions to help add to the corporate database, as discussed in Imperative 1. The knowledge base then supports future value growth.

Linking product and service is not new, of course. However, in the interactive Digital Age, it becomes more difficult to distinguish where one begins and the other ends.

With some of the new product offerings, the customer never touches anything tangible. And some service offerings can involve physical materials. Even with a physical product, the importance of one of our four A's—accessibility—can mean that how that product is made available can be seen as important as the product itself.

PRODUCT-SERVICE LINKAGES

Offerings that integrate product and service fall into five categories:

1. Service that surrounds product.
2. Service that encompasses product(s).
3. Service that is added to product.
4. Service that creates product.
5. Service that becomes product.

How products and services are best meshed into offerings depends on each individual situation. Following are examples of companies that took one of the five different approaches.

SERVICE THAT SURROUNDS PRODUCT

Bradesco, based in São Paulo, Brazil,[1] has redefined banking in South America by using new technology to accommodate a sophisticated urban populace with 2500 branches spread over 8.5 million square kilometers, including many remote areas.

As the first Brazilian bank to offer its services via mobile information technology, Bradesco allows its

Internet-connected direct banking customers (1.2 million of its 23 million customer base) to do their banking using their cellular phones, to send and receive e-mail messages, and to access other Web sites.

And that is just the start of the services Bradesco wraps around its traditional savings and loan business. Bradesco's InfoEmail allows clients to receive account statements by e-mail at specified customized intervals that the customer selects. InfoEmail includes an update of the customer's banking transactions along with daily news and comment on the financial markets, stock quotes, the dollar exchange rate, and other topics.

Customers can also make real-time stock trades online via the bank's brokerage arm, Bradesco Corretora. The bank's ShopInvest Web site creates a link to the São Paulo Stock Exchange's (Bovespa) home-broker online system for stock trading. Investors can send their buy or sell orders for stocks listed directly on the Bovespa, in real time. The bank can also collect the property tax in 48 Brazilian municipalities via Internet "Easy Phone Personalized Service. "

To provide their mobile services, Bradesco had to invest more than $1 million in cellular power systems at primary data-gathering and transmission points. Because of concerns about the reliability of the domestic energy supply, the company wanted to make sure that its systems would be able to avoid any breaks in power that would affect thousands of its mobile customers.

The investment illustrates a vital point: when you target a customer for whom "anywhere, anytime" service is important, you must go beyond merely setting up the service to ensure that it will truly be "anywhere, anytime."

This kind of commitment by Bradesco to providing customers with the information and support they want—

when and how they want it—has resulted in astonishing growth. The bank closed fiscal year 1999 with profit reported at $289 million, up 77.6 percent from the previous year.

Bradesco's role as a banker selling banking products is still its core competency, but the services that surround its products are the differentiator. The two now are insepa- rable, the banking and the service are the new offering.

SERVICE ENCOMPASSES PRODUCT

With everyone ultimately having access to anyone and anything at the touch of a button, companies are going to find it increasingly difficult to disassociate themselves from any element of the value chain.

Companies like Intel, which built its value in the ultimate consumer's mind with its "Intel Inside" campaign, can expect to be bombarded with e-mail if it even appears that a problem with a computer (which they didn't make) is related to, say, speed or processing.

While Intel's customers are the personal computer and digital appliance manufacturers, it now finds itself dealing with the final consumer of the product itself, even if the end product only "contains" an Intel chip. The company's product, in this case the chip inside the computer, has to be viewed now as a part of the product experience. When consumers buy a PC with an Intel chip, they expect Intel will support them.

For Intel, the product in the interconnected Net Future encompasses the implication of service.

Another company that finds itself facing the same issue is MasterCard. This is a brand known throughout the world for its credit cards, which sport its bright red-and-orange logo along with the name of the issuer of the card, usually a bank or financial institution. MasterCard has traditionally been behind the scenes doing the processing for the participating banks and financial institutions that solicit consumers to sign up.

In the past, if a consumer had an issue with the credit card, such as a card balance question or maybe a charge error, the bank itself was a logical place to go for resolution. The service relationship was with the bank, not MasterCard. The Net changed all of that, as MasterCard suddenly found itself in direct contact with the customer. In MasterCard's case, this means both merchants *and* cardholders.

"Cardholders and merchants are now coming directly to us," says MasterCard International President and CEO Robert W. Selander.[2]

> "This is a changing role for us. The customer now has direct and ready access to us because of our brand, which presents a significant challenge, because we don't want to disintermediate our real customer. When people think of MasterCard, they're thinking we actually do the price decision, which we don't. Now, when a person comes to our Web site, they have different expectations."

Manufacturing companies and just about any company with products sent to end users via distributors are facing the same challenge: "How to deal with our customers when our customers' customers expect they can come directly to us."

Suddenly, MasterCard has a product that encompasses a direct service relationship with the end user.

The issue of *disintermediation*—elimination of the intermediary, agent, or broker—is not new. However, in the Net Future the real opportunity is represented by reintermediation[3]—the networked environment provides more opportunity to play an increasing role in the value chain. It's when a company actually looks at where it can add value to others along the value chain.

This change in business-to-business relationships can forge a closer bond between companies and its distribution channel when handled creatively. This is what is happening at MasterCard.

MasterCard recognized it would have to adapt its Web strategy to be in line with its traditional business model, especially as customers began to expect they could apply for a card directly from MasterCard online.

Management decided to allow consumers to ask for a card online, but it kept its customers (the financial institutions) in the loop. MasterCard provides a list of banks or financial institutions to which the consumer can apply. If the prospect selects MasterCard directly, the application is routed to the appropriate financial institution automatically.

MasterCard now sends more than 500,000 completed credit card applications a year to its institutional customers. The end consumer gets what is "expected" from MasterCard, a full-service offering. And MasterCard's financial establishment customers collectively get a bonus 500,000 customers. Everybody wins!

Taking the built-in service relationship one step further, the company created the MasterCard e-wallet.

MasterCard wanted to leverage the interactive environment, with changing expectations and behaviors. Consumers were invited to subscribe to an e-wallet, either through one of the MasterCard financial institutions or directly from MasterCard itself.

The e-wallet allows consumers to shop online, more easily and confidently. When it comes time to buy, they click their e-wallet and have the purchase information filled in automatically, with the charge securely billed to their MasterCard. The logo of the provider, such as Citibank, Wells Fargo, or MasterCard itself, then "stays" with the consumer, so that's the logo on the screen as he or she visits other sites that accept MasterCard.

"When you think of 20 years ago, distribution and product were segmented. ATM machines were used for checking accounts," says Selander.

> "Product, distribution, and service are now a fundamental part of the customer experience. With the Net, Web phones, and PDAs, you can't separate them, because the customer expects they'll be able to use those devices.
>
> "Did people need 24-hour access to news before CNN? There is this appetite for freedom. We're expecting to have the freedom to do about everything everywhere you want, whenever you want. Whoever makes this transparent to the consumer has the advantage.
>
> "We don't want any of our customers to be disappointed when they think of MasterCard. We have to make sure there are no gaps in the delivery."

The company, headquartered in Purchase, New York, also proactively extended its reach to its customers with an online program that consumers sign up to receive e-mail offering special deals on products and services of specific interest to them. "You pre-sort yourself in advance. More than a half a million people have already signed up," says Selander.

Whether a company is delivering a financial product or is in a business with physical products, having the product encompass the service can be a way to better link not only with the consumer but with suppliers, distributors, and business partners as well.

SERVICE ADDED TO PRODUCT

Many companies are finding that the service added to a product strengthens the product offering and increases customer loyalty. It also helps to change the brand perception and the customer experience.

What many companies fail to realize is that from their customers' viewpoint, their products, services, and brands often are viewed as one entity.

Customers want a bank to know who they are. In reality, they are more likely to discover that one person knows they have a checking account, another knows they have a savings account, and still a third person knows that they have a mortgage there.

Too often, the bank is organized around its products, not its customers. This is how many companies grew up. A product was created; when it succeeded or failed, another product was created.

Unfortunately for many companies, it's only the customer who has corralled all the relevant company-customer relationship information into one place: his or her brain. The result often is a less-than-optimal customer experience.

One way to change this is to add a useful service to a product immediately after the launch. This can dramatically enhance the value of the product itself, while also enhancing the customer experience.

For example, Fidelity Investments, the largest mutual fund company in the United States, found that adding desirable services to its products—specific investment vehicles—was critical to the success of the products themselves.

The philosophy is part of the company's history. Fidelity got its start as the financial powerhouse it is today by allowing investors in money-market funds to write checks drawn against their accounts. Making it easy for people to take money out, the company reasoned, would make them more likely to invest it in the first place. It did. The fund was not the offering; the ability to write the checks was. The line between product and service became blurred.

In the Digital Age, Fidelity continues to understand that its customers look at the company not as a series of products, but as "Fidelity."[4]

"The product is the concept and the service is how it's being provided to the customer day in and day out," says Steve Elterich, President of Fidelity E-Business.

To assure that it approached the Net Future consistently, Fidelity handed the reins to Elterich. Elterich previously worked in the 401k area of Fidelity, with a background blending IT, product planning, and marketing. He was tapped by the COO to lead the e-business strategy.

> "Service is about somebody being able, if they have a question about how to open a new account at Fidelity, to get information easily and quickly.
>
> "For example, financial planning is a product for us. Once we launch the product, we continue to look at new features. But as the customer needs help from individuals as they use the product, that is service."

And in the eyes of Fidelity, service becomes more than simply answering questions. It is intrinsic to the offering.

Elterich notes:

"Providing a speedier Web site is even a service function, although marketing people might not be interested in that aspect. Look at Yahoo! It's easy to navigate, easy to get around. That's one of the reasons it's so successful."

Fidelity is an excellent example of how a company stays focused on launching a smart new product and then quickly turn it into an offering.

"The product is where you get two months of glitz at launch in the marketplace. If you don't have great service backing it up, it fails," says Elterich. "In the future, the service is the long-term sustaining capability. Service is going to be the area customers come back to," according to Elterich.

What does it take to succeed in such a role? "Strong personal relationships throughout the organization as well as the backing of the office of the COO," to whom Elterich reports directly.

Getting customers to come back because of the relationship provided is an essential of the Max-e-Marketing platform.

Here are some other examples of companies that add services to products to create offerings.

- To create and maintain loyal customers, McDonald's Corporation offers not just hamburgers at many locations but also enhanced customer experience. With McDonald's PlayLand concept, it turned fast-food dining into adventure and play for young customers and a respite for their parents.

McDonald's has also taken the fast food business into philanthropy with Ronald McDonald Houses— hospital-adjacent, home-away-from-home accommodations for young patients' families.

The most memorable McDonald's customer experience in Latin America has absolutely nothing to do with food. In Paraguay, where penetration of computers into households is extremely low, McDonald's has installed a number of computer stations in its fast-food outlets.

- Accessibility and wrapping services for their products have been part of the offering of catalog giant LLBean since its beginnings. Its 24/7 retail outlet in Freeport, Maine, continues to be a vacation highlight for travelers to New England, and it will still resole Maine Hunting shoes and boots at nominal charge for life. Sign on for an LLBean credit card and receive free shipping on catalogue clothing orders, complimentary product monogramming, and points toward gift certificates for merchandise. Forgot or lost your points certificates that came in the mail? No problem. LLBean also keeps track of them in their computer system and will honor them without the physical certificate. When they get near their expiration date, LLBean sends a gentle reminder that you are about to lose an opportunity to save money.

- Online or via telephone, give Florists Transworld Delivery (FTD) the name of a recently deceased person and his or her city and FTD will locate the mortuary or funeral home where flower arrangements should be sent.

- Gateway Country has led the way with showrooms for its computer products and peripheral equipment. High-touch, hands-on experimentation in a helpful, customer-friendly environment offers a memorable brand experience. You can try computer models, ask questions, make your selection, even buy a T-shirt.

• For Mercedes owners experiencing problems on the road, emergency help is a GPS signal away. Press the INFO button and you're speaking to a Mercedes specialist through the satellite system. Press the SOS key and Mercedes figures you're in trouble and help is on the way through the on-board GPS system, which precisely locates your car within seconds. And, when the airbags are deployed, a signal is automatically sent to Mercedes call centers so they can dispatch emergency vehicles. The service is totally integrated with the product to present a complete emergency road service offering.

SERVICE CREATES PRODUCT

In some cases, it is difficult to develop a personalized customer experience. When the average transaction dollar volume is too low—under, say, $20—capturing and maintaining customer information might be too expensive a proposition. However, service can become the mechanism for actually altering the value of the transaction.

When Garden.com began analyzing its online customers by their experiences and behavior rather than by traditional demographic segments, it came up with very different ways of targeting specific market segments.

Using a methodology developed by Net Perceptions, the company identified customers by "behavioral clusters," meaning groups of people who had similar experiences or who tended to behave in similar ways and who therefore had similar needs.[5]

For example, one such group might be people who entertain outdoors. Another, they found, were first-time gardeners. The company developed an online service that allows a novice to enter the dimensions and other specifics about his or her plot of would-be garden. Based on that information, the service not only lays out a suggested landscape plan but packages all the products needed to implement the recommendations. All the customer has to do is click one button to purchase everything that's needed.

In this case, the service actually developed the product: a personalized garden. A novice gardener might have approached the project piecemeal over time, an entirely different and less satisfying garden-creation experience.

Instead, service created a product offering that not only upped the transaction value but also provided lots of instant data about the customer's gardening interests, thus boosting the transaction value even further.

SERVICE BECOMES THE PRODUCT

When newly created, recurring service exceeds the value of the core product, it becomes a "platform." The *platform* is a consolidation of the product and service offerings in such totality that the complete experience actually becomes more valuable than the individual product that might have been at the starting point.

An interesting example of the service becoming a product is the program developed by MRM Budapest, the relationship marketing agency for the H&K Bank in Hungary. The bank created a portal Web site for children up to the age of 18, with many entertaining and educational features.

There is an obvious competitive advantage to starting a banking relationship during the early impressionable years of a young person's life. To get the relationship going, H&K offered "virtual bank accounts" at the site for participants who register. Then, as the various features of the Web site are accessed, whether through chat rooms, games, or educational areas, virtual "money" is earned by the young person. The more traffic at the Web site, the more "money" is deposited into the account.

And it's not entirely virtual. Withdrawals from the "cyber-account" can be made to "purchase" gifts ranging from pens, caps, and playthings up to a small-size TV.

In order to participate, children under 14 must open a real bank account at the H&K bank with their parents' participation, and teenagers over 14 can open a real-world bank account of their own.

The service—a virtual bank for the children's market— becomes the product in the minds of registered participants as much as the actual bank account that is opened in order to accept the offering.

THE 7 STEPS TO DEVELOPING AN OFFERING

1. What is your product?
2. Who is the consumer of your product?
3. What are that person's interests?
4. What else does your customer need or desire?
5. How can you provide it cost effectively as part of the product offering?
6. How can you help your customer understand the full value of this new offering?
7. How do you use the service relationship to capture more information?

LEVERAGE THE PRODUCT-CUSTOMER RELATIONSHIP

Established companies have a great advantage when it comes to creating offerings. This is simply because they already have the product and a relationship with the customer. In many ways, the opportunity is theirs to lose.

The quickest way to do so is to fail to take advantage of chances to use customer information to drive the development of individualized offerings. Because they have been in business for so long and have well-known brands, the best companies start with a profound understanding of their customers and a trust built up over decades. Analyzing customer data can easily become second nature in the transformation of products into offerings.

Ironically, a company can frequently fall short at the most unexpected of times, such as when business is good and sales are on the rise. That's when companies lean toward creating and introducing the obvious new products, rather than looking at existing relationships and products to find less costly ways to add services that enhance the value of their customer relationships.

Because developing more products may require new manufacturing equipment or plants, it is easier in good times to simply throw money at an opportunity rather than analyze how to take advantage of an existing customer base.

Conversely, when times are tough, existing customers suddenly become more precious. At those times, the money often isn't there to do expensive new acquisition efforts, and companies fall back on customers whose acquisition costs were paid a long time ago.

The key to leveraging the product-customer relationship is to reexamine what the customer actually is looking for in making the purchase. Is it a product or an experience? A thing or a result?

The answer to that question may lead to surprising offering possibilities. When a person contacts Hyatt or The Westin to book a room, it's a product that is being selected. In this case, a room for a night. But the offerings from each of these hotels with similar rooms might be very different.

A traveler could be offered the convenience of completing an airline reservation, car rental, theater tickets, and even tee times during that one call or online contact. What matters most to the traveler? The room? No, the trip! The room is only one component of what could be a powerful offering—not to mention a superb chance to show that the hotel is ready to exceed expectations by being genuinely helpful.

Leveraging the product-customer relationship requires approaching the market holistically, with no real distinction between product and related services. Applying this Max-e-Marketing imperative in the fierce competitive landscape of the Net economy is a winning strategy.

A true offering is an outgrowth of the relationship between a business and its customers. It then serves as a platform for reinforcing the relationship and generates behavioral information that contributes to making each relationship as different as each customer, as discussed in Imperative 3.

NOTES

1. The following is based on the authors' experiences and interviews in Brazil, where both authors regularly visit.

2. The following is based on the authors' interview with MasterCard International President and CEO Robert W. Selander.
3. The issue of reintermediation is more fully explored in Chuck Martin's *Net Future*, New York: McGraw-Hill, 1999.
4. The following is based on the authors' interview with Steve Elterich, President of Fidelity E-Business.
5. The following is based on the authors' interview with Steve Larsen, Vice President of Net Perceptions.

Make Each Relationship as Different as Each Customer

Add Relationship Equity to Brand Equity

The golden rule for business generally has been to sell as much of the same thing as possible to as many different people as possible. As production and distribution efficiencies increase with scale, the bottom line increases.

Back in the twentieth century, the concept of "customization" might mean producing more red cars because more people seemed to be buying red cars. It was almost entirely product focused.

Typically, customization would refer to what a company did with its offering to better meet the needs of certain groups of customers. The larger the customer group, the more likely the company would be to make an investment in "personalization."

In the new era of individualized marketing, everything changes. A company's products, services, prices, and customer contacts must become as varied as the customers themselves.

As companies move from customized products to customized relationships, the implications are immense. Among other things, the change reinforces the fact that in a wired world, customers are in charge, and any relationship must be established on their terms.

Looking at the "Use What You Know to Drive What You Do" imperative, when the customer is in charge, customer knowledge becomes critical. And as companies apply customer knowledge to each customer interaction, the outcome can be a unique experience for each customer.

Each of those experiences, in turn, can help to build a unique relationship between a company and its customer, who can be identified by name and personal behavior. For those who know how to take advantage of it, these newly formed relationships have a value that can be as powerful as brand equity in unlocking the potential of the business.

Developing an individualized relationship with a customer has been a desirable goal since the mid-1980s when the book *MaxiMarketing* was first published. But the pace of the technological change that has transformed manufacturing, distribution, and communication has finally brought companies to the point where the dream of being able to provide the right product for the right customer at the right price at the right time can become a Net Future reality.

Technology has been able, in some cases, to lower the costs of modular customized production to the point that economies of scale can be achieved without force-fitting each customer into the same box. Companies in the past have talked about "getting close to our customers," but "customers" was always plural. New technologies will enable companies to get close to *each* customer, as data-based relationships across all touch points become responsive over time to each individual's behavior and changing needs.

How is it possible and affordable to create one-of-a-kind relationships with customers by the thousands...by the millions...by the tens of millions...or even by the hundreds of millions? It begins with "Making Everything You Do Add to What You Know" about the customer and then harnessing the most advanced digital tools of the Mobile Information Age to put customer relationship marketing at the heart of customer relationship management.

E-CRM: GETTING CLOSER TO EACH CUSTOMER

Customer relationship management was the precursor to the new marketing approach of the new century. At first, it amounted to little more than a salesperson's contact software—a list of names of people to contact in order to sell them something. But, in the late twentieth century, as CRM began to employ an array of high-tech applications touching on every aspect of the customer interface, customer relationship management was wired into the total e-business architecture. With the arrival of the Internet, CRM evolved into *e-CRM*, an umbrella term for utilizing all kinds of software to manage sophisticated processes for impacting sales, customer service, and marketing.

The Relationship Marketing "four I's" of e-CRM involve:

- *Individualized marketing*: The ability to identify your best customers and deliver the right message to the right person.

- *Integration across channels*: The ability to create a consistent customer experience across all touch points, both online and offline.

- *Information- and technology-based empowerment*: The ability to use customer knowledge and customer interaction to provide customized offerings at a reasonable cost.

- *Internet-driven relationships*: The ability to use the Internet to maintain and deepen a mutually rewarding, brand-centric involvement with the customer.

The difference between winners and losers in the twenty-first century often will come down to who best handles the convergence of customer knowledge and customer interaction—powered by new customer care software applications.

With the mastery of e-CRM, a company moves:

- From selling the same thing to as many people as possible to anticipating demand and supplying the right thing to the right person in the right way at the right time in the right place.

- From setting a fixed price for the buyer to pay to dynamic pricing reflecting current marketplace forces.

- From following yesterday's tried-and-true business practices to doing whatever it takes to gain an advantage in a topsy-turvy world.

- From giving lip service to "putting the customer first" to making genuine attention a top priority.

BUILDING A RELATIONSHIP BRAND

Where does the one-to-one marketing hype end and the real world begin?

At the start of this decade, there were still very few Internet companies able to fulfill the promise of truly customized marketing because the technologies for delivering it are just emerging.

Even the pace-setting innovators at Amazon were willing to acknowledge they had a long way to go before meeting their goal of creating an individualized store for every customer who visits the site.

Over the next several years, the technology and strategic communications know-how to power the transition to responsive, interactive, relationships will gradually catch up to the promise. Those Max-e-Marketers at the forefront of experimentation with these new tools will be the "first movers" to reap the biggest rewards.

The message delivered used to be determined by fitting a customer into a predetermined category or profile of other customers with similar characteristics. Those profiles were based on aggregated behavior of those customers with comparable profiles.

Subsequent contacts with members of the group may have been personalized, but the personalization was tailored to all members of the group. Now, increasingly, new technologies will permit companies to respond to a customer's past behavior by personalizing future interactions with that person, based on that customer's characteristics and experiences. And as businesses move into a world of real-time interaction, each change in behavior can be tracked and used to drive additional sales.

That personalized interaction will be used to create a uniquely responsive relationship between brand and customer. It is that relationship that will come to characterize a brand, as much or more than the perception of product benefits characterizes it.

While the products of a company will come and go, the relationships created between company and customer can establish a lasting bond. In the Net Future, the enterprise will set a high value on its "Relationship Brand" based on what customers expect in the way of personalized products and services and from a true connection with those to whom they choose to give their loyalty.

Building the future value of a company's relationship equity falls into three categories:

1. Customized products leading to a one-of-a-kind relationship
2. Customized services leading to a one-of-a-kind relationship
3. Customized communications leading to a one-of-a-kind relationship

CUSTOMIZED PRODUCTS FOR ONE-OF-A-KIND RELATIONSHIPS

When Levi Strauss introduced mass customization of its jeans (originally Perfect-Fit and now called Original Spin), it brought the concept of forging a one-of-a-kind relationship to the apparel industry. The system enables a consumer to have jeans tailored to his or her measurements and to have the perfect-fit jeans delivered within a couple of weeks. With this one-of-a-kind relationship, the repurchase rate for customized jeans reportedly tripled.

Although Levi Strauss ultimately ended its e-commerce efforts because of high costs, it leveraged its relationship brand by making inventory information available on the Net so that consumers could find exactly what they were looking for at a store near them.

The customization strategy of Levi Strauss and other pioneers has been applied in a variety of industries since then. For example:

- Following the customization process introduced by Dell Computer, Compaq now offers customers the ability to design their own computers, either by using a special design station at a retailer such as CompUSA or Office Depot or at home via the Web. The company leveraged its existing distribution network rather than going the direct Dell route.

- Mattel allows a child to create a customized Barbie doll by selecting hair color, dress, and other features. Some doll makers can even scan a photo of the youngster's face and transfer it onto a doll's face.

- Listeners can download music to create customized CDs or order them online and have the CD delivered to them loaded with the songs requested.

- Web portals and financial services Web sites from My Yahoo to My Amercian Express encourage users to create a one-of-a-kind Web interface.

There's almost no limit to how far a company can go in creating personalized products. Nike has gone beyond just customizing the product; it now provides one-of-a-kind branding. With its Nike ID Web site, the company lets customers build their own shoes by choosing type of shoe, shoe size, gender, base color, and accent color.

More important to the relationship brand, though, is the customers' ability to create a unique name for their shoes by selecting a text logo and logo color. For example, buyers can brand their shoes as "Rebel" or "Outrage" or "Lovable"—whatever the heart desires.

If a company has spent millions of dollars to build a brand, as Nike has, why would they allow and even invite customers to, in essence, destroy it by adopting a brand of their own?

Because what is being branded has shifted from product to relationship, a customer may put the "Rebel" brand on the shoe alongside the Nike swoosh. But Nike's brand equity is now enhanced by offering the ability to have a one-of-a-kind relationship that lets a teen define his or her image *through* Nike rather than adopting an image sold *by* Nike.

And once a customer has given Nike the customer information necessary to create the Rebel brand, he or she can easily obtain more personalized "Rebel" products in the future.

A dramatic side benefit is that Nike can leverage all the time and money spent on setting up the customization process. How about expanding its unique branded relationship with other items such as sport apparel? In theory, Nike could even go beyond apparel to other demographically suitable product categories. Imagine offering a Rebel-branded portable CD player to play those custom-created CDs!

One very smart move Nike made in its initial introduction of the customized athletic shoe was to limit production. The company set a limit of 400 pairs of shoes for sale at a time in its first offering. People who came to the site too late were simply given a message to come and try again another day. There is nothing like "limited quantities" to generate an even more powerful urge to be the first to try a new thing.

The Nike ID site is a profitable e-commerce site that a spokesperson says is "meeting its expectations." The relationship Nike is forging with its customers will undoubtedly outlast the shoes sold. Nike is dynamically using captured customer information to tailor not just footwear but a one-of-a-kind relationship.

SINGULAR BRANDING SELLING BEAUTY PRODUCTS

At Reflect.com, you can see the first serious attempt to use the Web as a beauty products customization channel. It actually creates one-off products for women, wraps them with unique, personalized services, and creates a different offering for each customer.

The company sells cosmetics, all of which are designed online by the customer, who begins the one-of-a-kind relationship by answering a series of beauty and lifestyle questions.

Everything about the products is shaped to the customer's specification—from the shade, texture, and scent—to the packaging design and the brand name printed on the label. Customers can even choose the colors of the Web site itself.

What else is unique about this company? It's backed by Procter & Gamble, the most respected name in packaged goods merchandising. In fact, that link is key to Reflect.com's way of operating, and it demonstrates how smart marketers think about capturing and using customer information.

The data gathered from the customization process is extremely valuable to Procter & Gamble, which uses it as primary market research to understand what makes a person buy or reject personal-care products. It is information of value not only to Reflect.com, an Internet brand, but also to Procter & Gamble's many beauty care products sold in traditional retail channels.

The slogan "a product branded with you" is quite literal, says Rich Gerstine, Vice President of Marketing at Reflect.com.[1] The company goes far beyond ordinary personalization to establish an intimate relationship with its customers and uses the knowledge gained in a considerate way.

Says Gerstine:

"When you treat a customer as an individual, it's no longer marketing, it's a relationship. If a customer creates a product and doesn't like it, we will re-customize it free of charge. We also don't charge for shipping. We believe a truly loyal customer is someone who's an evangelist for the brand.

"We have made the decision to keep customer service and fulfillment in-house. We want to own all those touch points. We want to be able to control every aspect of the customer's experience."

By now you have probably heard some of the many new job titles being created to reflect the importance of customer relationship in the Net economy. But here is one you have probably not heard before. Reflect.com has an executive with the title of Director of Customer Delight, whose job it is to focus on reinforcing customer loyalty. The Director of Customer Delight came up with the idea of sending an orchid to every customer 3 days after that customer's order goes out. "They don't know it's coming, and it comes as a surprise," says Gerstine.

> "We think people respond better to that surprise than to, say, a button that says, 'For a free gift, click here,' and sets up expectations that can be disappointing. It's a very cost-effective way of marketing."

While giving away products, such as orchids, after a purchase may seem costly to you, Reflect.com looks at everything done for the customer from a traditional profit and loss point of view.

"Our experience shows that people who receive the free gift are three times as likely to re-buy as people who haven't received an orchid," says Gerstine. "They also spend three times as much money. The orchid program is a very cost-effective way of marketing. Compare the cost of orchids to the cost of buying a TV spot!"

Beside the postpurchase orchid program, Reflect.com goes a step further to try to win prospects who normally would not have been converted to buyers.

When someone creates a product but decides not to buy it, Reflect.com mails a sample of what they created anyway— at no charge. Gerstine states:

> "The product has her name on it, and that really comes as a surprise. We've gotten tremendous response from this. It's also a way of learning more about the factors involved in the buying decision."

PUTTING THE ERM (ENTERPRISE RELATIONSHIP MANAGEMENT) FACTOR INTO THE REFLECT.COM BUSINESS MODEL

Reflect.com is an excellent example of a company "using what it knows to drive what it does." Everything it does continually generates more knowledge to drive its future decision making.

But the business model of Reflect.com involves considerably more than gathering customer information and selling more products. As many Net start-ups and established companies moving into e-commerce have found out, closing the sale online is just part of the business process.

Reflect.com had to create an affordable way to manufacture a different product for each customer and even filed for a patent on its customized manufacturing process. Reflect.com looks at its business process holistically, linking everything from customer contact all the way back to product creation and the manufacturing infrastructure.

"The Internet is truly what has made this sort of personalization process feasible," says Gerstine.

> "It's a cost-effective interface, so it's easier to capture the customer data. The data is transferred to a neural network that develops a specific formula based on that data.
>
> "We have an integrated manufacturing system that makes the actual product based on that formula. The entire process means that we don't have a two-year inventory sitting around."

The knowledge transfer doesn't stop inside Reflect.com. "Because we are backed by Procter & Gamble, we also provide them with a new way to do test-marketing," continues Gerstine.

"We can get very rapid feedback on something and share that information with them to help them do better marketing campaigns. However, we have a strict privacy policy; individual customer information is never shared with anyone."

Will the Reflect.com business model turn out to be the breakthrough site that opens up a new era of mass customization? Only time will tell. What is certain is that Procter & Gamble is gaining invaluable know-how every day on how to run such a business. And that knowledge will become the foundation of the next evolution of mass customization in the Net Future. Established marketing innovators, such as Procter & Gamble, are continually finding new ways to leverage the learning of their Net start-ups. In the case of Reflect.com, a dramatic new testing mechanism was created for a real-time world.

Reflect.com is learning how best to maximize its gathering of information, and then use that information to drive the development of a one-of-a-kind experience. When fully executed, it's a strategy that owns the marketplace because there are no competitors offering the same unique product and relationship.

Apparel, computers, Web sites, beauty products, and almost any offering can be customized. Who is next? We believe some of the most interesting one-of-a-kind products in the Net Future will come out of the publishing world.

Any world traveler knows the feeling of having to tear out pages of restaurant listings to avoid packing an entire guidebook on France just to find a great place to eat in Cannes. With a program from iUniverse and IDG Books, travelers can select the sections of a *Frommer's Travel Guide* that pertain to their specific trip. You can create a customized, printed guide that deals only with your destination or interests. Like Nike, IDG and iUniverse are developing a branded relationship built on empowering you to create your very own one-of-a-kind product.

CUSTOMIZED SERVICES FOR ONE-OF-A-KIND RELATIONSHIPS

In addition to one-of-a-kind products, you can create one-of-a-kind services to solidify customer relationships. Because services on the Web so often involve digitized information, we are seeing a wide range of personalization in what is being offered. What follows is a sampling of what is out there:

- Banking is being transformed around the world. In the United Kingdom, an Internet bank called Smile has reinvented itself around a range of customized services. The customer-centric focus is the reason for the unlikely name. Smiling is possibly the last thing a twentieth-century depositor would have expected to do in a bank. But Smile is doing well as a twenty-first-century bank. The Smile metaphor works its way through everything it does to make the customer uniquely appreciated.

- Citibank in Australia offers personalized information about the weather, sports, community events, travel, news, shopping, and, oh yes, online banking. As with most major financial institutions, such as American

Express and Fidelity Investments, customers are invited on the home page to "first start by customizing this site to your individual requirements."

- Many financial services companies offer investors the ability to customize a real-time online ticker to provide real-time quotes and updates on the stocks that interest them. It wasn't that long ago that individual investors had to contact their broker for any stock quote to place a buy or sell order. Charles Schwab, America's leading discount broker, already is providing customized interaction on the Web for millions of its trading customers.

- C/Net allows consumers to enter specifications and price ranges for office equipment and computers. The service then locates models that meet those specifications and compares prices available.

- BankRate Monitor enables anyone looking to invest in a certificate of deposit to find the lowest CD rates in the United States.

- If you're a portal or destination site, e-centives offers an online promotional service that gets results by delivering the right offer to the right targeted consumer at the best possible time. If you're a merchant, advertiser, or manufacturer, e-centives lets you deliver customized promotions to prequalified databases of consumers across its Partners Network, your own partner network, or at your own site.

- Bank of Montreal was a leader in allowing prospective homebuyers to enter information about their income level, current debt, and length of mortgage to find out what price home an individual can afford to buy. A prospective homebuyer can also apply for the right mortgage for that person online. By allowing consumers to calculate their financial needs, such as how much they can afford to borrow on a car or a house, the financial institution also captures knowledge useful for customizing future contacts.

If there is enough incentive provided to get individuals to enter the kind of information about themselves that permits customization, the company achieves two things:

1. It captures valuable information that can be used separately and in the aggregate to provide exactly what the customer wants in the way of meaningful products and services.

2. It puts the power of inertia on its side. Few customers will want to switch and repeat the process elsewhere (assuming the original business relationship does an adequate job). Inertia translates into customer loyalty.

CUSTOMIZED COMMUNICATIONS FOR ONE-OF-A-KIND RELATIONSHIPS

Wireless devices and PDAs create a "walk, talk, click, beep" environment, in which a customer can be reached anytime, anywhere—at a location where the mobile device offers a connection to the Web. In the Net Future, most mobile devices will be equipped with global positioning systems that pinpoint where the user is at any given moment.

By combining this geographic information and the ability to deliver a message at exactly the moment that someone is likely to be most receptive to it, you can imagine almost anything becoming possible. Taken to its extreme, someone with a cell phone with global positioning could be in a mall about to walk past a favorite retail store. The store would have the ability to beep the customer at that precise moment (with permission) to point out an item on display in the window or on sale inside.

By using the store's customer database, the retailer could identify for sale a suit by a designer whose clothes that person previously purchased.

And, while we allow our imagination to run wild, in a real-time world, the store could offer a discount on that item that is good only for the next hour in order to lure the customer into the store immediately.

Such immediacy also would have enormous implications for a retailer's ability to capture data about the effectiveness of a given promotion and modify it on the fly. In effect, promotions would be constantly improved by constant real-time experimentation.

Sound fantastic? No more so than imagining five years ago that more than five million items would be up for auction every day in cyberspace.

WELCOME TO THE NEW AGE OF EXTREME MARKETING

Here is another scenario of Max-e-Marketers making each relationship different in the Net Future, utilizing multiple sales channels to satisfy customer needs and increase sales:

Consumer Kristen Nadeau goes to Tower Records' Web site to check out a Garth Brooks boxed set. It's expensive, so she adds it to an online wish list, thinking she might get it later. When she does put a Shania Twain CD in her electronic shopping cart, a message comes up notifying her that it's in stock at a Tower store a mile from her house and asking if she would like to pick it up.

Kristen is given the option of paying for the CD while online or at the store; she selects the store. When she picks it up, she notices that there are three coupons printed on her receipt for CDs that have been selected, based on her browsing behavior on the Web. One of the coupons is good for 20 percent off anything, so she decides to order that expensive Garth Brooks boxed set and have it delivered to her house.

When Kristen gets home, her daughter Emma asks her if she has remembered to get something for her grandmother's birthday, which is a couple of days away. Kristen thinks that the Garth Brooks CD set would be perfect for grandma. Kristen calls Tower's 800 number, where the customer service rep knows about what she just ordered. Kristen says, "I specified second-day shipping, but I just decided I want it FedExed to my office and gift-wrapped." The next day, while she is in a meeting, Kristen gets a message on her beeper from Tower. The message says her assistant signed for a delivery at her office and supplies the tracking number.

Everything in this scenario can be done today; it's simply a matter of implementation.

We call this futuristic concept of customized superresponsive *"extreme marketing."*

Extreme marketing will get a boost from technology, as processing power increases and prices decrease. We have already discussed GPS technology, such as what is used in GM's On-Star system. This same technology is appearing in handheld devices, such as cell phones. Add disposable chips that transmit their location, and we can envision another extreme scenario:

Arthur Kefalas has been looking at new shirts at the Saks Fifth Avenue Web site, but hasn't gotten around to buying. While at the Web site, he signs up to receive any new sales or product information. A few days later, as he's walking by the local Saks, his handheld device goes off. He looks at his device and there's a message: "Look up and to your left." He finds himself staring into the Saks window and sees on a mannequin the shirt he's been looking at online. The shirt has a transmitting disposable chip, so the store knows its exact location, and Arthur has a GPS in his handheld device, so the store knows he is passing the window at that moment.

A message comes to his device that says if he goes into the store right now, he will receive a 30 percent discount on that shirt. An electronic confirmation message is sent to a clerk in the store.

As he enters the store, Arthur's handheld device leads him along: "Go to the third aisle and take a left, and there will be someone waiting for you." Arthur complies, and finds himself facing a smiling salesperson with the shirt in his exact size at the counter.

"We've been instructed to give you 30 percent off this shirt, Mr. Kefalas. In addition, we understand that your two children like Britney Spears, is that right?"

"Yes."

"It just so happens there is a Britney Spears concert scheduled in the city where you live next month. We took the liberty of reserving four tickets, for you, your wife, and your two children. If you decide to purchase those tickets now, we also have been authorized to give you a 20 percent discount on the new Britney Spears CD, which I have right here."

"You are really something else!" Arthur exclaims. "Let me think about it."

"That would be fine. In addition, we've taken the liberty of sending an e-mail to your son Christopher mentioning the concert."

At that moment, Arthur's cell phone rings.

"Dad, can we go?"

And like most other things that are "extreme," companies need to take extreme caution in execution and implementation of what is possible and always protect the privacy concerns of their customers. However, executed correctly, the company-customer relationship can be dramatically enhanced, because customers welcome a relationship that gives the ultimate in personalized service.

We are only now entering the era of "extreme" customization in marketing communication. DVR personal video recorders marketed by Ti Vo and Replay TV and the new personal radio channels delivered to your car by Sirus satellite radio will give you total control of what you see and hear. You can make a DVR recording of any program—past or present—with one push of a button without setting a timer. You can pass up what is offered now and go back to any earlier Seinfeld episode. You can skip commercials at the press of a button, or ask for just certain commercials.

In effect, you will be creating your own one-of-a-kind programming.

GETTING CUSTOMERS TO TELL YOU WHAT THEY WANT

Permission-based e-mail has rapidly been adopted as a pillar of the new marketing that allows companies to target their promotions to precisely the customers who are likely to be interested in a particular offer. How do you know the customer's interests? Simple. The customer has already indicated what he or she wants to receive information about.

In some cases, the permission to be marketed to is given in exchange for rewards. In other cases, the customer simply wants to limit exposure only to information about products or services genuinely needed.

An entire industry has sprung up to explore the possibilities in this area. Here is just a partial list of the customized e-mail providers already battling for share of the market (each comes with its own particular variation to the theme): e-Dialog, Net Creations, ClickAction, Digital Impact, User Trends, yesmail.com.

Direct marketers, who have traditionally been at the forefront of targeted marketing, have been quick to adopt the new methods. But increasingly it's there for everyone to use.

For example, one large U.S. brewery that sent out an e-mail campaign to addresses obtained mostly from the company's Web site saw a 70 percent clickthrough rate— the measure of how many people clicked on a link to the brewery's Web page—from the campaign.[2]

Another example of a new e-mail marketer from a traditional industry is J.C. Whitney, which uses permission-based e-mail to sell auto parts.

When someone has given a company the OK to send them messages, chances are the customer will be more receptive to the message and the mailing will get a much higher response rate than postal direct mail. Companies also have to be attuned to when a customer says "stop" and is not interested at a particular time in a particular product or service.

The relationship is strengthened when the company listens and doesn't fall back into the "Sell! Sell! Sell!" mode.

Because the customer has, in essence, said, "Please send me information about this subject," the exchange is converted from a sales pitch to a service call. Permission-based e-mail reverses the communication flow between company and customer. Converting a "sales pitch" to a "service call," when done well, can support a company's effort to bond with the customer while asking for the order.

CUSTOMIZED COMMUNICATION ON THE CHEAP

The usual cost of reaching a customer via traditional direct mail can range from 50 cents to $2.00. The cost of an e-mail campaign is somewhere between 1 and 4 cents apiece and there is little limit to its scalability, according to Gregory Slayton, President and CEO of ClickAction, the agency that handled the beer campaign mentioned earlier.

Another e-mail campaign ClickAction conducted for a large direct marketer of apparel produced $900,000 worth of sales within 5 business days. The cost of the campaign? $15,000.

The process of registering to receive e-mail offers an opportunity to capture additional information that can be used to help understand the market better in the aggregate as well as individual customers. The registration form on a company's Web site is a marketing research bonanza.

ADD RELATIONSHIP EQUITY TO YOUR BRAND EQUITY

The evolution of company-customer relationships can be seen in the microcosm when you look at the airline industry. In the 1980s, airlines segmented customers by how much they flew, awarding free trips for people racking up miles.

In the 1990s, with the expansion of niche marketing, the airlines began providing special services for the most profitable niches. Some airlines met high-mileage travelers at the gate and shepherded them through baggage claim. Fast-track customs clearance and other special privileges became commonplace for the most desirable traveling customers.

In the first decade of the twenty-first century, the airlines have the ability to personalize treatment much further. They can—and do—know who is a jazz aficionado, a soccer fan, a vegetarian, or a contributor to the Shakespearean Society in the United Kingdom. To retain the most valuable relationships, the airlines will be moving to the next level of personal attention.

Sometimes personalized treatment is invisible to the consumer. Airlines have the ability to sort phone callers by how profitable they are. The most profitable business travelers, who book directly with the airline, instead of through a travel agent, can be routed to the top of the phone queue so that their calls are answered first.

All of this customization of products, services, and communications with and for the target audience adds up to the opportunity to customize the very relationship itself. Vast databases with constantly growing sophisticated customer profiles and dazzling new info-tech tools add up to the dawn of a new era in relationship branding.

Customization for its own sake is merely technological showing off. But if you use personalization to create a unique experience that brings the customer back time and again and encourages the customer to tell friends about the extra value benefits offered, the profitable return on the relationship keeps growing. And that greater value translates into both greater "share of wallet" per customer and greater market share as a whole.

NOTES

1. Based on the authors' interview with Rich Gerstine, Vice President of Marketing at Reflect.com.
2. Based on the authors' interview with Gregory Slayton of ClickAction, who conducted the campaign.

Do as Little as Possible Yourself

Others in the Net Economy Can Do It Better

In the Net Future, every company needs to think like Tom Sawyer.

In Mark Twain's novel, Tom's aunt assigned him to whitewash a fence as punishment. Tom beat the system, though. He realized that the best way to get out of doing the job was to make the task seem so appealing that he could get his buddies to do the work for him. Once he had assembled his team, Tom merely had to stand back, sip lemonade, and supervise. The work got done faster, and Tom had motivated his team to take pride in their work.

Doing as little as possible in your own company and getting other companies to do for you what they can do better is a key component of success in the new economy. Doing so not only allows a company to move more quickly—essential in the new marketing environment—it also takes advantage of highly specialized expertise in many different areas of new technology. And unlike Tom, you won't be conning anyone into doing the work. You'll be creating a support network of outsourced services provided by syndicators who have as much to gain as you do from this new business model.

Business Week, in its special issue on the twenty-first-century corporation, pictures the future as "organized around networks, not rigid hierarchies, built on shifting partnerships and alliances, not self-sufficiency."

This is counter to the dominant trend of the industrial era, when businesses often tried to do as much as possible in house. Vertical integration was believed to be essential to maximum profitability. Consider Ford and General Motors, for example. Ford at one point went so far as to own the rubber plantations that made the rubber for their tires. Until recently, General Motors owned (among other enterprises) Delco, EDS, and GMAC Financing.

The motive was not merely to supply a superior customer experience by controlling as much of the automotive manufacturing, sales, and distribution process as possible but it was also to be able to gain a competitive advantage and retain profit every step of the way.

Flash forward 50 years. At the turn of the new century, GM, Ford, and Daimler Chrysler formed a major collaborative effort. All three want to handle their combined $750 billion annual procurement using the Net. And they are combining forces at a single, horizontally focused Internet connection to streamline the supplier purchasing process.

Instead of profiting by doing more themselves, the "big three" automotive companies are looking to maintain profitability by making it less expensive to do business with the myriad suppliers who do much of the work.

For most companies, it is counterintuitive to allow outsiders to do what was once considered to be vital corporate customer relationship management work. The sense that "we are working for the customer" implies that "we" should do most of the heavy lifting to make things easier for our customers.

Yet, in the Net Future, it may make more sense to ask who should really be doing the work. Information rather than physical goods is the stock in trade of the Net economy. In a world where information is never consumed, an unlimited number of people can use the same information (software) provided by a single syndicator. Not only is it often smarter to let other companies or even your own customers provide solutions; in many cases doing so is essential to survive and prosper. As we move into the Net Future we increasingly see new proprietary technologies that let companies do more for customers more quickly, more efficiently, and at a lower cost. To succeed, a company must be ready to do as little as possible by having others do as much as possible—the heavy lifting—or be the niche provider itself so that it can profit from selling what it does best to others.

TEAM SOURCING FOR MAX-E-MARKETING SUCCESS

The Net Future is an interconnected business world in which companies can no longer afford to invest in each new wave of enterprise resource planning (ERP), customer relationship management (CRM), e-commerce software, and the latest information technology. It makes more sense to capitalize on the hard work of those who choose to specialize in each vital module and assemble what you need to build your own proprietary business model.

For years, the major consulting firms have been advising companies to focus on their core competencies. One survey shows that most companies are moving in that direction by outsourcing at least one corporate function. (See Table 4.1.)

Table 4.1 Functions Outsourced by Companies

Has your company outsourced any of the following corporate functions in the last year?

Function	Percentage of Respondents That Have Outsourced
Procurement/Purchasing	13.3
Human Resources	13.3
Information Technology	34.1
Finance/Accounting	16.5
Legal	22.9

Source: Net Future Institute research.[1]

As can be expected, with its myriad of complexities, the most outsourced functions were in the IT arena. The survey also showed that it is not only cost savings that companies are looking for, but rather cost savings in combination with improved efficiencies. (See Table 4.2.)

Table 4.2 Reasons for Outsourcing

Why Was the Outsourcing Done?	
To cut costs	4.7%
To improve efficiency	28.7%
A combination of the two	66.7%

Source: Net Future Institute research.[2]

Many companies from the bricks-and-mortar sector choose to enter reciprocal relationships with a dot-com company that can provide for the established company an e-business function it needs to operate more efficiently.

We call this concept "team sourcing." It occurs when the outside partner or partners become so involved in a vital part of the business that it ceases being a vending relationship and becomes a strategic business alliance. It also provides both parties with opportunities for developing benefits that go beyond the relationship itself. Every member of the team can gain from cross-referrals.

At first glance, team sourcing looks a lot like what happened with outsourcing. But, on closer examination, it becomes clear that online team sourcing can be automated, standardized, and speedily concluded in a way that handing off a process in the past never could match.

Team sourcing often goes beyond simple vendor-customer relationships, creating partnerships that are so interconnected that they can begin to resemble the closeness of the old, vertical integration model.

Team sourcing is done not only to cut costs but also to improve effectiveness. If specialized access to expertise can lead to greater productivity or the ability to capture an emerging market, simply cutting costs does not look as important as it used to in the Industrial Era.

INTERLOCKING STRATEGIES DRIVES TEAM SOURCING

When a company chooses to do as little as possible by turning to the right syndicator, it is usually for strategic reasons, rather than a matter of convenience. Net Future Institute research shows that 80 percent of established companies are willing to enter an equity relationship with one or more dot-coms.[3] And both sides recognize that there are many benefits for each partner. More than 40 percent of companies surveyed said they would enter into a tightly linked arrangement only if it were mutually beneficial. They ranked their considerations in order of importance (from most to least) as shown in Table 4.3.

Table 4.3 Things to Consider Before Entering into an Equity Relationship

1. Complementary or competitive product set

2. Relationship's impact on your company's future strategy

3. Win-win situation

4. Access to state-of-the-art technology

5. Gain of leverage from the dot-com's infrastructure

6. Elimination of other established companies from the relationship

7. Liquidity

8. Need for a stop-gap measure while ultimate strategy is decided

Source: Net Future Research.[4]

E-marketplaces in many cases involve equity arrangements. For example, when VHA Inc., a cooperative comprising 480 hospitals and 1300 acute-care institutions throughout the United States, wanted to help its members to make purchases online, it turned to a Net start-up, Neoforma.com.

"We signed a 10-year agreement because they specialize in health products," says Daniel Bourque, Group Senior Vice President of VHA.[5]

The core business of not-for-profit VHA essentially is group purchasing for its hospital members. Within a few months, VHA hospitals were moving more than a billion dollars in sales through the venture. One-third of its members were expected to join within 6 months of launch.

"We expect all our suppliers will offer their supplies on the exchange, then hospitals will go to the site to purchase, and a transaction fee will be paid by the suppliers," says Bourque. "We're using the Net as a tool to help our customers and our business partners to improve their efficiency and their relationships."

In return for the 10-year deal, VHA received a 35 percent stake in Neoforma.com, and plans to share the stock among its hospital members, as an incentive to everyone to drive the business.

BECOME AN EXPERT AT CHOOSING EXPERTS

In the Net Future, Max-e-Marketers will become increasingly dependent upon team sourcing. With each new digital advance, marketing becomes more complex. It is not possible to become instantly expert at everything. For an established company, learning all the new ways to attract and keep customers can be a staggering and very expensive task.

As e-commerce opens up new opportunities to supplement the usual channels and reach out to new and broader markets, you will be hard-pressed to take advantage of every opportunity without simultaneously facing up to the need for substantial investments in internal support functions.

The good news is that you do not have to take the do-it-yourself approach. There are a vast number of e-services providers ready, willing, and able to step in and take charge of everything required.

In this demanding environment, the marketing manager needs to become an expert at choosing experts. The key is to identify what the company can do best and to let others do as much as possible—especially in operations involving rapidly shifting technology and automated tasks.

This has been achieved brilliantly already in regard to outsourcing accounting or payroll functions. Now, to succeed in the Net Future companies will need to follow the team-sourcing approach to optimize every aspect of strengthening customer relationships.

WHEN MAX-E-PARTNERS CARRY THE LOAD

At first glance, many team-sourcing partnerships appear to be a new form of vendor relationship. However, for Max-e-Marketers, they represent much more than a contractual arrangement to supply a missing process or function. In many cases, the partnership is so integral to a company's success that it is difficult to tell where the company's public image leaves off and the vendor's takes over.

There are four types of hand-offs that can lighten a company's workload by getting the "heavy lifting" done elsewhere: (1) the process partner, (2) the relationship partner, (3) the behind-the-scenes partner, and (4) the self-partner. Each is discussed below.

THE PROCESS PARTNER

In an era when a unique distribution method or communication platform can become more important than the product itself, the process partner can help to focus a business on what can truly add value to its business model. This often involves helping with the process of establishing better customer relationships rather than the product. It is discussed in greater detail in "Make Your Interactive Process Become the Product," Imperative 5.

Office Depot provides the process that links its corporate customers to an automated office-supply procurement system. This system of intranets provides greater efficiency for the customers of Office Depot while helping to lock them into a partnering relationship.

Any cyber traveler who has bought a computer or a peripheral device or joined a club or signed up for special benefits at a Web site in the past few years has probably filled out a registration form. When a person does that, he or she fills out name, phone number, mailing address, e-mail address and answers a relevant set of questions. Obtaining this information, compiling it, and analyzing it is the "heavy lifting" job most often team-sourced to a company named Naviant. Charles Stryker is the CEO and innovator behind this fast-growing Web-based information resource.[6]

Stryker says:

> "Sooner or later every person on the Web is going to have to fill out a registration form and when you do we will handle it. If you agree, we collect your information and add it to our database. Once there, your information can be used for a number of very useful things. One way in which the customer derives direct benefit from this is the development of more targeted product information, so you are not sent sales pitches for a handheld device when you just purchased one from another company a few months ago.

"The information we centralize as a single unified source is being used to dynamically change Web content to suit the surfer's preferences. When you log on to a Web site, it may be able to find you in Naviant's database and alter the content of what is being offered to fit your interests. From our marketing partner's perspective, the database offers a wealth of targeting data, updated in real-time and making available an e-mail address, a postal address, and often a phone number. You can't get all that in any old economy mailing list."

Other examples of process partnering:

- Net Creations has a database of millions of opt-in e-mail Internet users who have given permission to receive e-mail messages on one or more of 3000 topics of interest. Net Creations manages the opt-in e-mail lists generated by almost 200 participating Web sites that collect expressions of interest at their sites. Net Creations takes over the list and markets it, finding advertisers who want to reach those various profiles and freeing its "partners" to concentrate on the content of their Web sites while sharing in the advertising revenue generated.

- Toysrus.com, the e-tailing toy giant, teamed up with former competitor and e-commerce giant Amazon.com to build a joint online toy store. Toys "R" Us turned over its inventory-handling and warehousing to Amazon to take over handling transactions and filling orders. Toys "R" Us continues to do what it does best, assemble the hottest toys and gauge demand six months in advance. Together, Toys "R" Us and Amazon are writing the new rules of the team sourcing for selling toys on the Net.

- Ace Hardware has linked FindMRO into Acenet 2000, the hardware distribution company's intranet. The affiliation gives Ace's 5000 store managers a way to locate any product consumers want. The Ace "partnership," along with a deal with ENI-Net.com, an e-marketplace for the environmental industry, helped catapult FindMRO from $6 million in orders to a $50 million-per-year order rate.

The syndication of the complex searching process in many different forms promises to become a big business category of its own in the Net Future.

THE RELATIONSHIP PARTNER

Relationships can take a long time to build—time that often is simply not available to a business. Any company that has won the confidence of an enormous existing customer base can help out less fortunate companies. Often overnight, by providing access to its database with appropriate compensation, the owner of the relationship figuratively outsources the connection to its customers, and everyone involved benefits. We call such companies "relationship intermediaries."

American Airlines is an example of a pacesetting relationship intermediary in the airline industry. The AAdvantage frequent-flyer program is the world's largest mileage-accumulation affinity program with 40 million registered members. By affiliating with more than 1000 program partners—everyone from hotels and rental car companies to real estate brokers to sellers of mutual funds, to roofing contractors and the local dry cleaners—American provides multiple means for its registered frequent flyers to log points redeemable for travel and other awards.

The AAdvantage program has three roles: (1) encouraging flyers to use American for the miles, (2) targeting promotions based on information in the AAdvantage database, and (3) offering access to its database to partners that buy the "miles" they use as a purchase incentive to customers. "We want to spread the ubiquity of the currency, so that people can use their miles as currency to buy other stuff," says Bruce Chemel, Vice President of the AAdvantage Marketing Program.

To enhance the process, American Airlines teamed up with America Online to let members earn miles when making purchases online from AOL. The program also allows AAdvantage members to combine cash and miles to get trips, and to purchase a wide range of products online from AOL.

American Airlines also sells blocks of miles to small businesses. A business can then issue mileage vouchers to customers or send its mileage records electronically to American Advantage. These relationships benefit from having these customers become part of the largest and longest-lasting affinity program in the world ("I'll get miles if I buy from them"), the potential for gaining phenomenal customer knowledge, enhanced loyalty from program members, and the credibility of linkage to a famous brand name.

AA benefits as well. On average, roughly half the frequent-flyer mileage awards redeemed represent partnership mileage, for which AA is paid 2 cents or more per mile by the partner company. In some cases, the airline can make more from the "free" ticket (based on the 50 percent paid by the partners) than it might be able to collect from selling a heavily discounted seat. To the consumer, the frequent-flyer trip is free, but for American Airlines, the AAdvantage program reportedly generates an overall profit.

As Chemel indicates, the huge concentration of AAdvantage partners also helps establish AAdvantage miles as, in effect, an alternative currency. The more partners, the more ubiquitous that currency—and therefore the more travel is encouraged on AA. The airline hopes to increase the value of mileage currency by making it easy to use mileage to buy anything from books to grocery products; AA has already run a successful program with "miles" offered in exchange for buying Kellogg's breakfast cereals.

"I used to wish I could use my miles for anything I wanted, but that wasn't feasible. There was just no way to do it until everyone became connected by the Web," says Chemel.

At the American Airlines Web site, frequent-flyer members are experiencing a new level of convenience in placing reservations, obtaining last-minute discounts, and monitoring participation in the program. Before long, the Web will afford 40 million Americans an unending list of purchases made possible with AA mileage currency.

Other examples of relationship partnering:

- The auction service EBay is a relationship intermediary providing instant access to an ever-expanding worldwide universe of both buyers and sellers. Sellers write the classified ad for the merchandise offered and handle shipping; buyers bid for merchandise and pay the seller directly. EBay creates the marketplace for both, in exchange for a portion of each transaction. The auction participants team up with Ebay, the outsourcer of a process that allows electronic bidding and establishes a trusting relationship with tens of millions of buyers and sellers.

- First Tuesday.com has found a way of linking venture capitalists and entrepreneurs. It sponsors gatherings at local bistros worldwide at which entrepreneurs get the opportunity to meet with people who might be interested in investing in their e-ventures. Entrepreneurs are identified by green dots on their name tags, investors by red. It's a relatively quick way of screening possibilities for both sides and getting a relationship started. What's amazing here is that what started as an informal networking party in 1998 at the Alphabet Bar in London's SoHo has become a worldwide phenomenon. When First Tuesday was introduced in Buenos Aires, Argentina, 40 would-be entrepreneurs and venture capitalists attended the first meeting. The next month, 80 people showed up; the next month, 160. By the summer of 2000, the company had to rent a disco to handle the 2500 attendees. The people who came up with the idea later took to the Web and plan to make money by taking a cut on the deals that emerge from the events.

Not every company that starts down the relationship partnering road has the daring to follow the AAdvantage example. One such example is the International Health, Racquet & Sportsclub Association (IHRSA), which comprises members from the management of 5000 health clubs from around the world.[7] It includes members from well-known facilities such as Bally Fitness, Gold's Gym, and 24hourfitness as well as lesser-known local facilities.

But no matter the size of the club or fitness location, the industry is primarily a membership business, relying on regular dues and sign-up fees. With their attractive demographics, members of health clubs are attractive to marketers with health and fitness products.

The company spent several months looking at organizing an e-marketplace for its members, but found too many problems in potential execution.

"It was really too risky for a small organization," says IHRSA Executive Director John McCarthy. "We studied it and decided not to do it. We decided to leave it to the big guys, it was too risky for us."

With access to the heads of all the major health and fitness centers, IHRSA would have had the opportunity to introduce its strategy and build consensus at the annual forum of its membership leadership.

"The closer you get, the more challenges you see," says McCarthy. "It's very tough to do."

THE BEHIND-THE-SCENES PARTNER

In contrast to the team sourcing (discussed previously), a behind-the-scenes partner often handles a very narrowly defined aspect of the business. Its capabilities are so invisible to the customer and so intertwined with the company's future that the relationship cannot be easily broken without severely damaging either the product offered or the value chain.

The behind-the-scenes partner can perform functions needed to expand a partner's business or provide capabilities never imagined. For example:

- Hong Kong Mass Transit and Kowloon-Canton railways allow passengers to travel with a stored-currency, contactless smart card. AES Prodata, a global automated fare-collection systems company, designed and executed this smart-card fare-collection solution which is backed up by an essential uninterrupted power supply (UPS) from Powerware Corporation. AES Prodata and Powerware provide the behind-the-scenes activities that furnish Hong Kong Mass Transit with the ability to serve 10 million customers daily with state-of-the-art systems that speed both work commutes and routine city travel.

- ImproveNet, an Internet site designed for consumers seeking comprehensive home-improvement information and services, offers several services that reduce expensive estimating time for contractors and manufacturers. For example, the site's Roofing Estimator service provides precise cost analyses of roofing materials and installation, establishing those particulars before contractors are called to a site.

- Amazon.com's Associates Program, begun in 1996 as the first program of its type on the Web, invites other Web sites to offer links to Amazon.com to facilitate purchases from Amazon's extensive offerings. Some corporations immediately began recommending specific books to employees on their corporate intranets. Fulfillment by Amazon was just one click away, and a percentage of the profit on each book ordered goes to the corporation. Amazon.com now has several hundred thousand other sites in the associates program. Why go to the trouble of selling books yourself when you can have the world's greatest online expert, Amazon, do it for you?

Especially in areas that involve advanced technology, many companies are turning to behind-the-scenes application service providers (ASPs). These companies allow their clients to pay a monthly fee to handle a proprietary-function. With the emergence of ASPs, it became much easier to rent each new automated business solution instead of buying expensive hardware and software for attempting to do it yourself.

Solutions that are delivered by an ASP generally are housed at a central location, then transmitted via the Internet or a dedicated line to companies that lease the software. Many business technology suppliers that have traditionally provided sizable companies with software and equipment are beginning to look at supplying full-service, behind-the-scenes solutions.

- Oracle, which specializes in software for large databases, especially in the financial arena, has developed Business OnLine as its behind-the-scenes B2B enterprise resource.

- SAP, which has led the market for systems that help streamline the manufacturing process, created MySAP and ultimately partnered with Commerce One to work together on digital e-marketplaces.

- PeopleSoft is taking the same approach to human resources functions such as benefits and payroll.

- The Boots chain concentrates on opening and running stores that offer low prices. However, a cornerstone of its marketing strategy is a loyalty program and a credit card that is state of the art. Rather than divert its resources to developing, installing, and maintaining decision-making database software, the company turned to Egg, the innovative UK direct bank, to supply the loyalty marketing component of the Boots marketing process.

- Marks + Spencer became a financial marketer overnight by partnering with Equitable Life, the behind-the-scenes processor of its financial services.

In the upcoming imperative on "Making the Brand Experience Exceed the Brand Perception," we focus on the "careware" providers that handle many different aspects of customer relationship management more efficiently than many companies could manage on their own. In the delivery of vital CRM components, a company such as iSky or Live Person is not simply a vendor; to the outside world it is the company.

THE SELF-PARTNER

In some cases, the business can market more effectively when it partners with a Net-focused unit within its own operation. Established companies in many industries are developing separate units of their own to participate in business-to-business exchanges. Such self-partnerships allow a company to participate in the supply chain while both buyer and seller enjoy a great deal of flexibility in the specific relationships formed when a deal is done.

For example, Tyson Foods, which processes 47 million chickens per week, partnered with food distributors Sysco, Cargill, and McDonald's to create the Electronic Food

Service Network, a supplier exchange to leverage its buying power.

HOW STAPLES DOES IT

Staples is a self-partnering company.[8] Like any other business, it must efficiently manage its procurement process—no small challenge when dealing with thousands of vendors of office supplies.

To streamline that process, Staples has adopted an automated procurement system developed by Ariba Technologies Inc. Staples has a retail arm, represented by both bricks-and-mortar stores and Staples.com, that focuses on small businesses and individuals. It has established a marketplace that offers 70 different categories of services for small businesses. These customers can either buy services at the prices negotiated by Staples or post a request for price (RFP).

Anne-Marie Keane, Staples Vice-President of Business-to-Business E-Commerce, says that being on both sides of the fence has helped Staples understand the benefits and challenges of the new e-marketplaces.

Here, in her own words, is the Staples self-partnering business solution:

"What Staples did internally on the process side was to develop a workflow process that looked at the activity-based costs of e-procurement. We identified what commodities had high volume, both in terms of transactions and dollars, to prioritize which commodities would provide us with the best savings if handled in a more automated fashion.

"The next step was to take each priority commodity and work out a process flow that tracked exactly what happened in the course of a purchase. In office supplies, we counted 21 steps that were involved in simply getting office supplies to someone who needed them. That's typical of a lot of companies. Office supplies is first on the list of things people want to handle by e-procurement, because it involves so many little items that are purchased so frequently.

"As a result of this analysis, we've now got a 3 to 4 step process. The requisitioner goes online to order the supplies needed. An individual approves the order after being notified by e-mail that there's a purchase request waiting in their approvals mailbox. The request and approval gets transmitted to the approved supplier, who delivers it. Finally, the results of purchases are analyzed by the purchasing team to look for usage and buying trends or unusual orders. The basic benefit of internal e-procurement is going online with your supplier. It's less time consuming. Depending on the commodity area, we found we could save 40 to 80 percent in process costs.

"Customers who are considering e-procurement have three options, and none are mutually exclusive. They can buy directly from vendors online from a vendor's Web site; in our case, it would be Staples.com, Quill.com (for small to medium businesses), or StaplesLink.com (for large customers with corporate contracts). They can buy an internal procurement software system, such as those from Ariba or Commerce One. Or they can go to an e-marketplace, perhaps a vertical marketplace.

"Initially, we suggest that companies set themselves up to buy low-risk, high-transaction volume items online using their existing suppliers' Web sites. That way they can begin getting their employees used to online procurement and begin to realize some pretty significant savings while they're exploring or implementing other options.

"People shouldn't underestimate what's involved in moving to e-procurement. We did an informal survey of our customer representatives to try to determine the level of training that would be needed for our corporate customers' employees to do purchasing online. We found that 50 percent of the employees at our corporate accounts used computers but weren't used to the Internet. Ordering through a vendor's Web site isn't usually terribly complex in terms of setup. By contrast, setting up our own e-procurement software just at our headquarters took 10 months to implement.

"Companies that are contemplating participating in a marketplace need to think about how integrated they want to be with their accounts payable, with accounts receivable, and what kind of resources they have to do that. There is a lot of custom work that needs to be done to achieve that integration. So far, the networks that are out there tend to offer multiple suppliers, but then individual companies rarely put multiple suppliers on their own system; they select a company from the ones available on the network and put that company on their system.

"The fastest-growing piece on the sales side for us right now is the direct-from-supplier purchasing. Buying through procurement systems such as

Ariba's, that are installed at large corporations, represents about 15 percent of our sales. A lot has to happen for that to take off. Right now there's not enough volume or velocity to support all the marketplaces that are being talked about.

"With business-to-business marketplaces, people know that whatever they see out in the marketplace is not the final price they can get. They know that if they sit down with a vendor, they can get a better price. That's a pressure we deal with today.

"The experience of doing our own internal e-procurement opened our eyes to how important it is to plug into our customers' systems. Companies can't start achieving the savings of any system until their suppliers are up and running on them; the suppliers have to get plugged in quickly."

As described, Staples is both a self-partner for itself and a process partner with other companies. Many businesses follow more than one partnering model.

PARTICIPATION IN E-MARKETPLACES

ServiceMagic.com, a Web site backed by Maytag, Quest, *USA Today*, and Certainteed Corporation, creates a network of nearly 50,000 contractors and appliance repair specialists accessible via the Internet. The site provides users with names of professionals whose skills match job needs; users now take on the responsibility of scheduling home improvement or repair. ServiceMagic receives a $200 annual fee from professionals listed, plus a commission from completed projects booked via the site.

Net Future Institute research shows that such meeting places are becoming increasingly important as a way of getting what is wanted. In one survey, 88 percent of those asked said their companies were either in or plan to be in a digital e-marketplace in the future. (See Table 4.4.)

Table 4.4 What Is Your Organization's Current Level of Participation with Digital E-Marketplaces?[9]

We run one	25.3%
We participate in one	21.6%
We do not participate but plan to in the future	41.6%
We do not participate and do not plan to in the future	4.5%
What are digital E-marketplaces?	6.9%

Source: Net Future Institute research.

PUTTING SOMEONE ELSE BEHIND THE WHEEL

While many companies increasingly get others to do the work for various pieces of their businesses, others are just beginning to think about total business involvement. This happens when another company takes over and essentially runs the enterprise. Said another way, the contracted company does virtually *all* of the heavy lifting!

In the past, the Disaster Recovery division of IBM was called in when a disaster struck. A company would contract with IBM to make sure its data was safely stored in a separate location in case of a disaster, such as what would happen if a hurricane or earthquake hit the main facility. It was simple enough: the disaster hits, the company uses the other data center, run by IBM.

"In the 70s and 80s, it was all about 'provide me with a second environment where I can go if my environment is disabled,'" says Todd Gordon, IBM's General Manager of the disaster division which changed its name to Business Continuity and Recovery Services[10] to reflect its changing role in the new economy. Gordon continues:

> "In the new world, we're having to bridge between outsourcing and E-Business. Companies now are looking for some insurance or some enhanced value in keeping their business running. With wireless communications and pervasive computing, if it doesn't work, you have nothing for a business. Companies are looking for an end-to-end solution."

He goes on to say, "Post Y2K, the focus is on the people, not just the IT. Companies are looking for application continuity, then ultimately, business continuity."

During fires in Colorado, IBM deployed teams of human resources people, related government area managers for external communications, transportation, and logistical management. IBM typically deploys teams for between 30 and 100 events a year on a global basis, with free-standing resources in various countries totally focused on keeping a business running, no matter what.

One event involved a luxury car company that was hit by a flood at its call center during Hurricane Floyd. It wasn't that the company's technology failed; the employees simply couldn't get to the office. IBM basically flipped a switch and all the roadside assistance calls were automatically routed to pretrained call center staff who sounded like actual employees of the company as they dispatched help to stranded motorists. Yet another staff handled reservation calls for a major cruise line when its call center was disabled by the same hurricane.

"Customers are just starting to think about just what does it take to keep a business running," Gordon notes.

The IBM business continuity group also handles "fail over," which is what happens when a company exceeds capacity. A classic occurrence took place when Victoria's Secret advertised a fashion show on its Web site during the Superbowl. Everybody wanted a seat on the runway.

Gordon comments, "A lot of companies are just discovering that the impact of disruption from the Web is much worse than anything that might have happened before. Because if it's not working, the business is not there."

In essence, the emerging uses of the business continuity group illustrate the shift in brand value from the product to the relationship. What the IBM disaster group is protecting is not just a thing, but a company's three-dimensional relationship with its customers. When the relationship itself is threatened, a company is now ready to have IBM take over the wheel and drive everything.

CIRCULAR TEAM SOURCING

In some cases, team sourcing ends up being reciprocal. When Hewlett-Packard customers call the product support phone number on the back of a package, they are connected to an iSKY customer service professional, who might be in Canada. The entire process of troubleshooting and customer support has been turned over to a "heavy lifter" that knows best how to satisfy Hewlett-Packard's customers.

Each Hewlett-Packard customer's detailed transcripts of of previous interactions with the company are held at iSKY.

This allows each customer interaction to be tailored specifically to the individual needs of that person when an iSKY representative is contacted.

What makes the relationship reciprocal is the fact that Hewlett-Packard is one of the companies that provides computing systems to iSKY. Since iSKY does Hewlett-Packard's customer service, any iSKY employee who contacts Hewlett-Packard with a tech support question actually gets the answer from a fellow iSKY employee somewhere!

REAL-TIME MARKET RESEARCH

Even areas that have traditionally been outsourced, such as market research, will take on a different Net Future dimension in "letting the other guy do it." For example, when real-time data about actual sales patterns is fed directly to a company, it has effectively outsourced at least a part of its market research function to its customers and distributors rather than to a market research group that might conduct a statistical survey.

Vending machine companies have been experimenting with being able to change soft drink prices in real time to respond to weather patterns. When the temperature goes up, the company might charge more for a cool drink. Such information can also be used to do test marketing. Buying patterns can become the yardstick for measuring how likely customers are to be price sensitive. Rather than asking a group of people in a room with a one-way mirror, real-time data from a test group of vending machine locations serves as a de facto focus group.

In this instance the customer is doing the work of market research—without ever knowing it!

WHEN THE CUSTOMER CREATES THE PRODUCT

Another route to doing less is to use the customer as product developer. Some examples follow.

- One of the most cost-effective ways to let others develop the product is to use the customer base to create a product that lures other customers. Information-rich product development that has the credibility of real customer experience has been the basis of businesses such as About.com. It developed hundreds of what we call "experience communities"[11] by aggregating groups of people based on collective postings on bulletin boards and chat lines.

- About.com has hundreds of live "guides" that help consumers find what they are looking for. The richer the content, the better the product, which, in turn, attracts new community members that attract advertisers.

  "About's GuideSite business model has enabled us to create a platform of venues for advertisers that really is unmatched in the industry," says CEO Scott Kurnit.[12]

  "But it has also allowed us to be in the forefront of the Internet phenomenon where no matter how much technology becomes available, the desire to connect with a human being remains stronger. Merging the two and offering both advertisers and users this highly targeted experience is what distinguishes About now and in the future."

- The product reviews featured on CNET.com, which are written by professionals, are supplemented by the posted experiences of people who have bought the product already. That self-perpetuating feedback is part of what helped C/Net to grow to the point that it could acquire high-tech publisher Ziff-Davis' ZD Net.

Community-created products such as these use customers themselves to help form a bond between customer and customer—and as a result, between company and customer. The company becomes more than a maker of a product; it becomes the catalyst for interaction among like-minded people. In building that community, the customer input becomes the product itself for the "heavy lifter" that makes it happen.

WHEN CUSTOMERS HELP THEMSELVES

Companies often can satisfy customers better by letting them do some of the work. For example,

- Chevron Corp. is saving more than $10 million a year by letting franchisees help themselves to information about their accounts online. Gas station owners can check financial information as well as manuals and marketing brochures. The company also plans to allow station owners to order online. The self-service system is backed up by a call center that will help franchisees use the Web site.

- Dunkin' Donuts, Togo's, and Baskin-Robbins not only list any of the stores for sale throughout the United States but also allow potential franchise owners to do the work of applying for a franchise directly from its Web site.

- With $19 billion in sales, Sysco is the nation's largest food services distributor. To extend its brand and empower its business customers, Sysco provides them with an inventory manager and menu cost analysis system that can be purchased online, and provides technical support to those customers.

- Speednews allows major airlines to list and sell its used planes, such as L-1011s, DC-9s, 737s, and even 747s. At one time, 700 aircraft were listed for sale, along with 167 companies.

Of course, the flip side of customers helping themselves is that a company has to be prepared for a more informed customer. If there are operational issues, such as failure to maintain inventory levels, they will be more apparent than ever. When brand is based on performance, not promise, the process of delivering on customer expectations has to be flawless.

Once you have mastered the art of "getting others to do it for you," you are ready for the fifth Max-e-Marketing imperative: "Make Your Interactive Process Become the Product." In the days of Mark Twain's Tom Sawyer, doing as little as possible was a welcome thought. But who would have ever guessed then that the twenty-first century would bring us an "others-do-it" marketplace where the intangible becomes more valuable than the tangible.

NOTES

1. Net Future Institute survey of 1600 business executives throughout the United States and Canada in 2000.

2. Net Future Institute survey of 1600 business executives throughout the United States and Canada in 2000.
3. Net Future Institute survey of 2500 business executives in 1500 companies in 32 countries.
4. Net Future Institute survey of 2500 business executives in 1500 companies in 32 countries.
5. Based on the authors' interview with Daniel Bourque, Group Senior Vice President of VHA.
6. Based on the authors' interview with Charles Stryker, CEO of Naviant.
7. The following discussion of IHRSA is based on the authors' interviews with IHRSA Executive Director John McCarthy.
8. The following is based on the authors' interview with Anne-Marie Keane, Staples Vice President of Business-to-Business E-Commerce.
9. Net Future Institute survey of 2500 business executives in 1500 companies in 32 countries.
10. Based on the authors' interviews with Todd Gordon.
11. From the concept first introduced by one of the authors in *Net Future*, New York: McGraw-Hill, 1999.
12. Based on the authors' interview with Scott Kurnit, CEO of About.com

Make Your Interactive Process Become the Product

Now Is the Time for: The Process Is the Message

What company is not looking for sustainable (or at least repeatable) competitive advantage? This has been one of the most fundamental principles of business success for years.

Until now, this has meant capturing and holding customers so they wouldn't be carried off by a competitor. Consider some traditional language used by marketers: "barriers to entry" and "barriers to exit" are created. Companies create unassailable brands, trying to sear their products or service attributes into the customer's mind.

It's all about winning competitive advantage.

In the networked economy, however, the focus shifts from a product-focused advantage to a relationship-focused advantage. Although a relationship advantage may be more difficult to create, it can be more easily sustained in an era of product commodification.

A relationship advantage can be created in two ways:

1. By making the customer interaction process itself at least as valuable as the product or service—in many cases, more so.

2. By developing processes that leverage business partnerships and create networks that expand the value delivered to the consumer or a business customer.

Focusing on the interactive relationship process to gain competitive advantage essentially redefines what a customer is buying. Process is the way in which intangible benefits are conveyed to the consumer at every point of contact, both online and offline.

In that sense, e-commerce is not a revolutionary new development but rather an evolutionary extension of the direct marketing process, with its emphasis on intersecting smoothly and efficiently to deliver the right message about the right product to identified prospects and customers.

PROCESS AS PRODUCT FROM THE CONSUMER'S PERSPECTIVE

In some cases, successful companies have redefined entire industries by making their process drive the offering and become its competitive advantage. Amazon did it to become the premier e-tailer. Dell did it to become the number one seller of personal computers. There are many others as well, some in industries that have traditionally been product-centric.

Consider the case of Lands' End, the $1.3-billion, Wisconsin-based direct merchant of clothing for men, women, and children. Lands' End, which also sells soft luggage and products for the home, was one of the first top-rated catalog marketers to migrate to the Web at landsend.com. Lands' End started selling online in the early 1990s, back in the days of the early online service providers Prodigy and Genie.[1] In 1995, the catalog marketer moved its online efforts to the Web.

Lands' End is one of a handful of marketers that utilizes online shopping not only to benefit the consumer but also to add profit to the company's bottom line. The Lands' Ends strategy holds lessons for everyone about how to combine online and offline activities seamlessly.

"It was a classic start-up with a server in a closet and all that," says Bill Bass, Senior Vice President of e-commerce at Lands' End when asked how it all began. "We sold $162 in our first month online. We sold $5 million the next year, $18 million the next, $61 million the next, then $138 million the next."

Already the largest seller of clothes online anywhere in the world, Lands' End is well-positioned to continue doubling revenue annually, even though the company's online strategy does not involve competing on price or providing other than the usual retailing promotions and incentives.

Why is Lands' End so successful where so many others have had lackluster performance at best in e-commerce? Because the management has figured out that success depends not so much on the product as on the underlying process driving the interactions with the target audience.

And the process for Lands' End is all about the marriage of technology and customer experience in the online and offline worlds so as to enhance the technology-enabled relationship with its customers.

With its focus on creating a uniquely satisfying customer experience, Lands' End constantly rethinks the process management of all its contact points and finds innovative ways to surprise and delight its customers.

"Our first innovation was a personal model," says Bass. "You put in your measurements so it will look like you and then you try clothes on the model." Each person, in effect, creates his or her own cyber-mannequin.

During a 6-month period, 1.6 million women came to the site and created computer-generated models with their own measurements. They could then use their online facsimiles to "try on" merchandise, giving shoppers the opportunity to combine the convenience of catalog shopping with the confidence that comes from trying on a garment in a bricks-and-mortar dressing room before deciding to buy. Interestingly, Lands' End captures no information from the individual's sessions. "We're privacy fundamentalists. You have a lot of companies stepping on a privacy land mine. At our site you can be solitary. We don't track people around the site," Bass states.

This concern would at first glance seem to run contrary to the first imperative of Max-e-Marketing: make every interaction an opportunity to capture information. Clearly, there are times when protecting privacy takes precedence in building a relationship based on trust and mutual respect.

This underscores a fundamental principle of genuine customer care. It is not what you say, it is what you do in the Net Future. Yes, tracking people can provide a company with valuable information. However, there are times when the trust built by leaving someone alone can be worth far more than adding more data to a database that already contains a great deal of information about a customer's purchase behavior.

There is one area in which Lands' End wants to make sure the customer is not left alone: when the customer has a question the company must respond fast. So the next process innovation involved real-time customer contact. Bass explains:

> "When we first added online customer service, you could send us an e-mail and we would guarantee a response within 3 hours, though most came within 30 minutes. Companies have a hard time responding to e-mails.
>
> "The problem is, if you're shopping, waiting 30 minutes for an answer is terrible. We wanted to change the rules. We said, 'What if we come up with some kind of instant response?'"

Rather than invent a solution on its own, Lands' End got others to do the "heavy lifting." They called on Massachusetts-based Net start-up Webline to launch Lands' End Live, allowing shoppers to talk directly to a customer service representative while they shopped.

It became the first large-scale, one-touch access service for online shoppers. If a shopper has a question or a problem at the Lands' End Web site, he or she enters name and phone number and a customer service representative calls back instantly. "Our standard is to have a response to you within 20 seconds," says Bass.

That kind of dramatic improvement in customer care—from 3 hours to 30 minutes to 20 seconds—says a lot about how the underlying process drives the relationship that drives the company's success.

For Lands' End, enhancing the connection to the customer is everything. It's all about instant gratification and easy access. "We really look at what's going to make a better experience. Every year we try to come up with something new."

At Lands' End innovation never stops. The company found a better way for consumers to get recommendations for style, color, and what is most flattering for that person. Using answers from a short series of "which do you prefer most" questions, Lands' End is able to route people into a number of different customer segments and make helpful recommendations for them.

Bass says, "Eighty percent of our buyers are women, but only 50 percent of our product is for women. We have a lot of people buying gifts for others."

"I don't want anybody to provide a better customer experience than Lands' End," is what we heard from Bass. "I want us to be the leader in customer service."

The company is always looking at enhancing experience through new interactive processes. It introduced the "Shop With A Friend" program, which allows friends and family in different locations to shop together; each sees the same screens simultaneously.

With shoppers visiting its site from 184 countries it did not take long for Lands' End to set up a system to serve some customers in their local languages.

"We are one company, and however the customer wants to interact with our company we want to excel," says Bass. "The same photos used in the catalogs are used at landsend.com. Whether a customer orders a product by telephone, catalog, or over the Net, it goes through the same pick, pack, and ship process. The same customer service representatives, who average 9 years' experience, answer phone, chat, and Net-based live questions."

Lands' End is a model of how established companies can leverage their existing infrastructures and assets to create end-to-end processes for making a truly unique and caring experience. It is this combination of virtual and real assets that can drive any company, whether a manufacturer, a store retailer, or a catalog house such as Lands' End, into the "process-creation" business.

Whoever owns the platform for exceeding customer expectations in the Net Future has the best opportunity to bond with the customer and continually take the pulse of what is needed next.

It's not about moving a business online that matters, but rather about making the customer connection seamless and satisfying, no matter how a customer decides to deal with a company at any given moment.

In the case of Lands' End, whatever route the customer takes has its own special advantages, Bass says, "Graphics are better-looking in print than on a computer screen, but online we can carry every product in inventory. Catalogs are just a subset of the inventory."

During the last Christmas season, for example, Lands' End didn't include swimsuits in the catalogs; rather, it focused on the season at hand. As a result, catalog sales of swimsuits were zero. However, during that same Christmas season, the company found itself selling 300 swimsuits a week through its Web site.

"We try to make it as seamless as possible for the customer," says Bass.

At Lands' End, the process has become what makes the product so appealing. In effect, it is the product.

What Lands' End has accomplished demonstrates the advantage held by established brands moving to the Net. There are few pure e-commerce retailers that can leverage the infrastructure of a Lands' End in transposing the successful catalog direct marketing model to the Net .

THE AMEX INTERACTIVE ONLINE EXPERIENCE

American Express is another good example of an established brand taking advantage of its existing offline customer relationships to create worthwhile online brand-centric experience.[2]

American Express created an "offer zone" at its Web site, where cardholders can take advantage of specific offers.

For example, a cardholder in New York City can review various entertainment categories to find what he or she is looking for, such as a restaurant for dinner. The customer selects a particular restaurant offer and at dinner gets a special deal when paying with the American Express card. The entire process serves up a special additional benefit in being an American Express cardholder.

"The discount is automatically credited into your statement and the restaurant never knows you got a discount," says Anne Busquet, President of Interactive Services and New Business at American Express. "That's an example of a complete customer transformation, and we've improved the customer experience."

Several Net start-ups are attempting to create a business model for making online restaurant reservations, and must laboriously convince restaurants one at a time to sign up with their service. By contrast, American Express already has its merchant network in place—an enormous head start.

What is especially interesting about this example is that American Express has managed to transfer the goodwill of the brand experience from the restaurant to American Express itself. Ordinarily, the restaurant would provide a coupon, and the customer would turn in the coupon at the restaurant to get the discount. With the process devised by AmEx, as far as the customer is concerned, the discount on the bill seems to come from American Express instead of the restaurant.

"You have to transform the customer experience to make it better than what it used to be. Then the customer transforms behavior," says Busquet. And in the process of transforming that behavior, American Express has managed to solidify its own brand relationship with the cardholder. At the same time, the AmEx Web site and the automated architecture that handle the transaction helps drive business to merchants who accept the card.\

And American Express processing innovation doesn't stop there. There is the promise of a new ultimate level of privacy protection when you buy online with your card at the Amex Web site.

MARKETING TO THE NET-SAVVY

A generation that grew up with visual images will soon be superseded by a generation that is growing up not only with visual images but with an instantaneous connection to everyone anywhere in the world and everything anyone wants to know. This new generation has its hands on a keyboard or a cell phone pad punching out messages in response to text eagerly read for the information provided. The interactive connection mind-set has displaced couch potato mentality.

Almost half a century ago, when television announcer Marshall McLuhan said, "The medium is the massage," he meant that the way a message is delivered influences the content and perception of that message. TV required a very different approach to creating a marketing message than print had.

McLuhan was talking about the impact of change at that time. The move to graphic moving images that soon would reach most of America sitting and viewing TV screens evening after evening caused a fundamental change in the very nature of marketing. The medium, with its ability to impact the perception of a brand at an unprecedented low cost per impression, became the driver of the perception of the brand.

Now everything changes again. The new technology of the Net economy, and the increased savvy of today's consumer—and even more important, tomorrow's consumers—push the envelope of "the medium is the massage." Brand perception remains important but now, "the interactive process is the massage."

How do you market to an audience that is increasingly media-savvy, skeptical of marketing efforts in general, and with unlimited access to pricing and product information? In this new era, the process of how a product is marketed including every interaction with the customer (as Lands' End and AmEx have demonstrated) also becomes part of the brand message. Marketing strategies that simply attempt to establish brand image are doomed when customers interact directly at a company's Web site and have access via the call center, chat rooms, and ubiquitous e-mail to a 3-D view of the company and its offerings.

Brand experience is no longer limited to experience of the product or service alone. It extends to experience of the company as a whole. The future value of the enterprise is equal to the sum of the brand value and the relationship value—the aggregate contribution of all future customer interactions.

For the Max-e-Marketer, a marketing strategy without an interactive component is no marketing strategy at all. But that interactivity has to be supported by a process infrastructure ensuring a happy outcome for the customer.

Process as product applies not only to the marketing campaign but has an effect throughout the organization. Everyone who interacts with end users or the business customer is part of the relationship-building process. When the interactive process is the message, everyone in the company is a marketer, from the workers in the warehouse at Christmas time, to the call center programmers, the IT systems engineers, and the CEO.

PLATFORM AS BRAND

Michael Dell at Dell Computer Corp. understands the concept of process as product. In good measure it was this understanding that made Dell into the world leader in selling personal computers. Dell, which pioneered the concept of selling computers directly to consumers by phone, also was one of the first companies to use the Net as a sales channel. Dell now does more than half of its sales volume at its Web site, selling more than $40 million worth of computer equipment each day in cyberspace.

With a business model that has always been direct-centric, Dell easily moved from its successful single-channel model to an even more successful "channel confluence" model.

Dell's exceptional growth exemplifies all of the Max-e-Marketing imperatives. Dell uses what it knows about each customer to drive what it does for each customer. Dell's offering is both product and service. Dell makes each relationship different for business customers and the home computer user. Dell gets others to manufacture the hard drives, monitors, and other components of its computers. Dell makes its direct distribution interactive process its competitive advantage. Dell provides a brand experience that consistently exceeds the brand perception. And Michael Dell showed how to make the top corporate executives responsible for marketing and marketing responsible for the rapidly growing business year after year.

Dell specializes in designing and customizing products and service to the needs of its end users. Its extensive build-to-order operation can put together a customized computer within 24 hours of taking an order on the phone or from the Web. It was one of the first to use the Web to let users, whether at work or at home, configure and order their own computers.

Dell has been increasing its total quarterly product shipments at almost twice the combined rate of the industry's 10 largest companies. The performance becomes even more impressive against the backdrop of achieving sequential margin improvement. The company's unit sales growth runs at about 22 percent overall—even more in enterprise servers, storage products, and notebook computers.

Understanding its business customers has allowed Dell to offer a highly personalized brand experience. The company not only tracks service records but it also allows the customer to track online each interaction with the company. That service record is so fundamental to its relationship with customers that even at the manufacturing facility, a Web-based touch screen can track Dell's record on service and support for an individual customer.

The virtual customer record screen can be located anywhere in the company and the same information is available via intranet to the company's quality-assurance engineers.

INSIDE THE BUSINESS

Dell's early focus on direct interaction with the home PC user received rave reviews in *MaxiMarketing* when the company was little more than 10 percent of its present size. And it is that same ability to master the interactive process that now drives Dell's success in the business-to-business market.

Through a system called *Premier Pages*, Dell offers its customers a way to automate corporate orders. A corporate buyer can link its intranet to a secure, customized Web site hosted by Dell that allows purchasing and leasing of computer equipment. Each intranet site also provides one-stop access to service and support information specific to that company's computers. It includes reports about manufacturing, status of current orders, and listings of approved configurations. In 2000, Dell hosted more than 35,000 such Premier Pages.

What Dell did for the home PC buyer to create a totally new experience in buying a personal computer is now a totally new experience in the corporate world. Sales to the business market account for 65 percent of its overall revenues.

In selling to other businesses, companies often do not think of themselves as a direct marketer or a one-to-one marketer. In the Net Future, all that changes. "Being direct" in following the Dell Max-e-Marketing model is the shortest route to sales, profits, and building a corporate brand in a networked business environment.

THE ALLIANCE PROCESS FOR GAINING BUSINESS ADVANTAGE

Companies such as Lands' End, American Express, and Dell are not the only ones benefiting from the new emphasis on process as competitive advantage. Increasingly, every business must use interactive process technology to create advantage not only for themselves but also for the alliances they form. (See Figure 5.1.)

One of the most startling turnarounds in the Net economy is the way in which information sharing with traditional competitors can now provide a business advantage. In a world that is constantly evolving, the more people you have on your side—even if those connections are

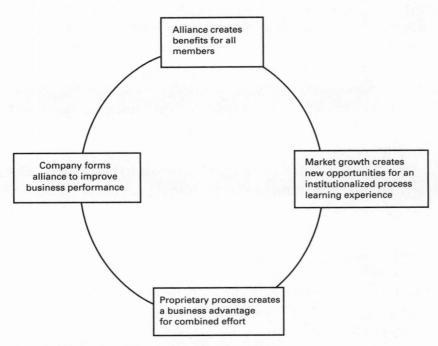

Alliance creates benefits for all members

Company forms alliance to improve business performance

Market growth creates new opportunities for an institutionalized process learning experience

Proprietary process creates a business advantage for combined effort

FIGURE 5.1 The advantage circle.

temporary and subject to change—the better chance you have of finding out what you need to know to survive.

Alliances have become the new currency of commerce, and companies who focus on building walls around themselves will soon be outpaced by competitors working together to build a more productive environment.

THE ADVANTAGE CIRCLE

Why is process and information sharing so important in the new world of advantage-by-alliance?

- *Business partners expect it*: Smart companies no longer measure success strictly by sales figures. In a world where resources are often strained to meet the business opportunities available, companies are looking not just for sales but for true partnerships that can add to a company's future value in ways that go beyond cash in the bank. Each new partnership formed usually brings with it the chance to expand the company's knowledge base.

- *Employees expect it*: In order to advance their careers, employees can no longer be content to focus solely on what their own company is doing. A highly fluid workforce increasingly will want to be able to work on projects that tap into cutting-edge technology and lead to career advancement and recognition in their fields. They will want exposure to colleagues who will stimulate their own thinking. Companies that provide staff opportunities for exposure to other experts in their field, even if it at times means collaboration with a competitor, will be the ones able to attract the best and brightest employees in the first place.

- *Customers expect it.* The world of the Internet connects everyone to everything. Customers are now accustomed to doing their own research before buying. What you will find increasingly at the center of gaining a competitive advantage is a reputation as the best source of trustworthy answers for customers. Your partners can be key to establishing that tight bond.

CMGI was an early example of a company that has created competitive advantage by enabling its network to form strategic alliances. Its portfolio of Net companies leverages one another's technologies and knowledge to help encourage the growth of online advertising.

Internet Capital Group has done the same in the business-to-business world. By investing in a number of different companies that can then share knowledge, resources, and technologies, it creates a network that can become a symbiotic facilitator instead of being just a motley aggregation of Net start-ups.

Max-e-Marketers in individual industries can take advantage of intermediaries that are focused on cross-industry platforms and also learn what works in industries other than their own. The market intermediaries, in turn, provide the cross-industry companies with a deeper understanding of their specific markets.

WALL STREET'S FOOTPRINT ON THE BRAND

Marketing in the real economy that bridges the Net and established channels means taking into account what Wall

Street thinks as part of the brand. With more and more Americans owning stock, how Wall Street rates a business becomes part of the brand image of the company.

With the increasing use of CNBC, CNNfn, and Web investment chat rooms, Wall Street's perception is an increasingly important part of Main Street's perception of the brand.

Stock price, a company profile in *The Wall Street Journal* or *BusinessWeek*, the discussion in ex-employees' bulletin boards—all are new factors in determining brand valuation. More than ever before, the company itself is seen very much like a product.

This means corporate management will be increasingly pressed to focus not only on the customer but on all of the stakeholders. Those stakeholders can include a company's customers, employees, managers, distributors, business partners, suppliers, and, of course, the shareholders.

The real-time brand experience of every stakeholder is overtaking yesterday's reliance on a brand image slowly built over time. It evolves into the key factor in determining brand perception and, ultimately, the purchasing decision.

BRAND EXPERIENCE LEADS TO FUTURE VALUE

A vital concept in Max-e-Marketing is what we call the "brand experience." It directly affects the relationship between company and customer and contributes to the long-term future value of the business.

Brand experience is created by a combination of satisfaction with the product (P) being branded, the interactive contact experience a customer has with it (C), and the interaction of those two elements over multiple contacts in multiple contexts over time (T). In other words,

Brand experience = (product quality + contact quality) × time

$$BE = (P + C) \times T$$

In the Net Future, the equation has yet another component, which is not as controllable: experience with others. What are others saying about your products? We live in a world where it is now easy for anyone to learn anything about a company's product. Every major company now shows its leading products at its Web site, and an e-pinion is always just a click away. As more customers interact with the companies they do business with, as well as other customers like themselves, the formula becomes:

Brand experience = (product quality + contact quality + other opinions) × time

$$BE = (P + C + O) \times T$$

In the Net Future, the customer is in the driver's seat. While a company may provide information through its sales staff (see Figure 5.2), that same customer has total interactive access to the company's other customers as well as information from direct competitors.

This puts more pressure on the enterprise to enhance the relationships it already has with existing customers because those people will either be helping or hurting potential future sales to other customers.

All these interactions, between company and customer, customer and other customers, and customers with competitors, contribute to the brand experience.

Contrast this with brand perception, which is created largely by one-way messages from company to customer.

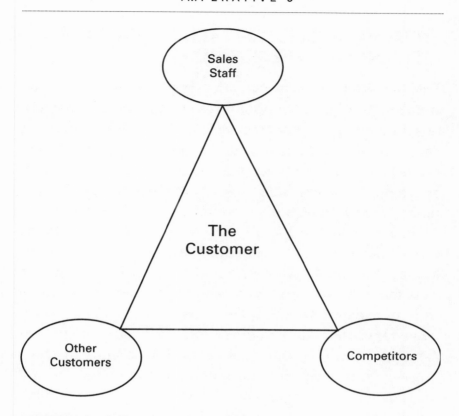

FIGURE 5.2 Spheres of influence.

But too often, the positioning images created by advertising copywriters and public relations departments are out of phase with the actual customer experience.

The time factor in brand experience can help mitigate a negative brand perception. For example, a superb customer service department can help offset a competitor's more positive brand perception. However, the equation is unlikely to work in the opposite direction. Few buyers are attracted to a product they perceive as falling short just because they know they can get service.

BRAND PERCEPTION VERSUS BRAND EXPERIENCE

The brand experience over the past few years with an Amazon, E-Bay, and Yahoo! have created a brand perception in the same league as McDonald's, Pepsi, Nike, and Ford, without substantial advertising expenditures. Word of mouth plus direct contact plus a uniquely satisfying interactive process architecture have built these companies in a relatively short time into powerhouses in their fields.

Because of the global nature of the Internet, these brands have the added benefit of having been, in essence, launched globally. Software that works here also works over there. More than 20 percent of Amazon's sales come from outside the United States. It is difficult to find a business executive anywhere who has not heard of Amazon.com. In addition, Amazon and other Net start-ups—even if not profitable—are continually watched by the media and management in various markets around the world. (See Table 5.1.)

Increasingly, what lies behind brand experience is the ability of automated software programs to provide an easy, reliable, consistent technology-empowered outcome. In the info-tech real economy, brand experience at times can be more difficult to manage than brand perception, and often has little to do with mastering the traditional four P's.

Priceline showed how a Web-based business can use a brilliant advertising campaign to enhance its brand perception. The campaign that featured William Shatner as spokesperson went off the charts in gaining brand awareness.

Unfortunately for Priceline, this happened at the same time that its attempt to have Priceline members set their

Table 5.1 Brand Perception Versus Brand Experience

Brand Perception	Brand Experience
Created largely by broadcasting one-way messages.	Created largely by direct contact.
More easily changed.	Once established is more lasting.
Developed by saturation, concentration, repetition of the brand message.	Often develops over multiple contact points and interactions.
Changes by changing the ad agency.	Negative experience is difficult to change.
Company has more control.	Company has less control.
Involves indirect feedback.	Involves direct feedback.

own price for the groceries they buy ran into consumer dissatisfaction with the process and had to be cancelled. Cancellation of the grocery discount club had a devastating effect on the Priceline share price, which then negatively impacted the brand image.

Brand perception was terrific; not so with brand experience. It is brand experience, not William Shatner, that will help the company fight its way back to stakeholder approval.

THE P911 PHENOMENON

One of the most significant aspects of the marketing process in the Net Future is that word-of-mouth marketing happens out of sight—specifically when it comes to children, who are continually marketing to each other online.

After school and in the evenings, parents can see their children online chatting with others like themselves. Millions of kids are "IMing" each other, sending Instant Messages to one another on America Online. The messages pop up instantly, and the communication that follows can be difficult for any adult to track.

When 11-year-old Ryan Martin comes home from school, he signs on to AOL to chat with friends Chris, Matt, and Michael. While "chatting," Matt tells Ryan he has just bought rapper Nelly's new CD online. Matt says it's great. Michael says he likes it, too. Ryan tells his 9-year-old brother Chase that Matt just got the new Nelly CD and he and Mike both like it. Next thing, Chase is asking mom and dad to buy him the new Nelly CD.

Many parents seem befuddled that all the children seem to want the same thing at the same time, from the latest Razor scooter to the new Beastie Boys CD. There is a private word-of-Net world that is invisibly operating in the background. It is a world into which parents generally are not allowed to enter.

We call this peer-to-peer marketing by children to each other the P911 phenomenon. Why? It's Net shorthand for "parental emergency." When any parent is in the room, the child types the code "P911," which tells all the other children online to be careful what they say, since a parent is in the room.

MAX-E-BRANDING

So, with so much changing, what do you do about branding in the Net economy? Here are a few thoughts for starters:

CONNECT WITH END CUSTOMERS

Know and reach out to end users by name and behavior pattern. Especially when selling through traditional reseller channels, companies need a mechanism for interacting directly with their ultimate customers. If a person's only experience with a company is through an intermediary, the product experience will be limited to someone else's performance and an impersonal "Does it work or doesn't it?"

In the Net Future, it becomes much easier for any company to establish a direct relationship at its own Web site. Consumers already expect it. The big challenge is in finding ways to bring prospects and customers to the site and introducing them to a genuinely rewarding experience that keeps them connected to the company's brand. All this must be done without disintermediating the role of the traditional distribution channel.

DROP BRAND BAGGAGE

In some cases the brand reputation that a company has worked so hard to develop over the years may actually be standing in the way of developing the right image in the Net economy environment. For example, when GTE decided to become Genuity and Bell Atlantic changed its name to Verizon, each gave itself a chance for a fresh start while actually tossing off the balance sheet the enormous investment in creating the brand equity in the GTE and Bell Atlantic names. What it got in return was the chance for a new relationship, a new brand experience that it expects will create even greater brand equity in the Net Future.

Ohio-based Symix, a 20-year-old company focusing on Enterprise Resource Planning solutions for manufacturing companies, created a subsidiary called Frontstep,[3] to focus on E-Business solutions. Within months, Symix changed its corporate name to Frontstep, making Symix the subsidiary!

TRY VERB BRANDING

It has been an article of faith among marketers that, whenever possible, companies should protect a brand by trademarking it. Once a trademark is established, it must be defended against all imitators or the company risks losing ownership of the mark.

However, in the Net economy, defending the name may not be the best strategy. In fact, it might be an advantage to actually attempt to make a precious brand name or even the company name into a cultural icon, used as a generic term.

Trademark usage has been notoriously difficult to control, anyway. Just ask Xerox, which has for years tried to prevent people from referring to the process of photo-copying as "Xeroxing."

In some cases, thinking about what a brand would represent as a verb can stimulate thinking about exactly what business a company is actually in. We call this concept "verb branding," where a company creates a platform so powerful that the activity of doing its thing supersedes the identity of the products themselves.

For example, a business associate recently said he wanted a colleague to have a copy of one of our books prior to a speaking engagement there. Since the talk was only 3 days away, he offered to "Amazon" the book to his colleague. He was talking about the fact that online retailer Amazon.com allows customers to charge merchandise and have it sent directly to someone else overnight via Federal Express.

Using the Amazon name as a verb probably gives Amazon's trademark lawyers fits. But listen carefully to the message that is being sent when someone talks about "Amazoning" that book. Amazon started as an online bookseller, and despite its efforts to expand that brand to other forms of merchandise, the company is still linked to books in many people's minds. In this case, our associate is not focusing on the purchase. He is talking about Amazon's process for getting the book to the right person quickly. It is a process that applies as well to the myriad of other things sold at the Amazon site.

What does this say about what business Amazon is in, what its true product is, and what its future business strategy should be? The brand value expressed in the use of Amazon as a verb directly supports the competitive advantage represented by its delivery and customer contact process. The speaker was saying "I'll Amazon it" in much the same way many people say, "I'll FedEx it."

The process has become the product. Implied in "amazoning" a book to someone is the belief that:

- It can be ordered with one click.
- It will be the right product.
- The sender will receive notification.
- The billing will be correctly charged to the buyer's credit card.
- A package tracking mechanism will be in place and available to the buyer.
- If there is a problem, it can be fixed by simply sending an e-mail to Amazon.com or calling customer service.

It is this processing platform that allowed Amazon.com to expand into selling other products such as CDs, toys, recreational equipment, electronics, and thousands of other items at its z-Shops. Jeff Bezos realized early that the customer experience was more valuable than the products themselves.

VERB BRANDING AS STRATEGIC THINKING

Thinking about how to verb brand a company can also give you clues about extended business strategies. To build on the previous example, the similarity between "Amazoning" something and "FedExing" it (apologies again to the trademark lawyers) might open up a strategic path for either company. It could lead to a truer picture of the business Amazon is in than any brand strategy focused on mere retailing.

Think about the concept of verb branding when considering acquisitions or partnerships. What combinations of companies would be of interest if your company were verb branded? Amazon is in the business of delivering value with ultimate convenience; what does this say about the power that an Amazon-FedEx combination would have?

If Amazoning makes sense as verb branding, what other examples might work in the future? See Table 5.2.

The argument against commodifying a brand is that it leaves a company vulnerable to price competition. If everyone is "Xeroxing" instead of photocopying, why not go with the company that lets you do it most cheaply? But aggressive price competition is a fact of life on the Net anyway. And as we have noted previously, the lowest price

Table 5.2 Examples of Net Future Verb Branding

	Verb Means	Why Established
To "Cisco"	To acquire appropriate companies and integrate them into the existing organization smoothly.	Cisco has grown through making smart acquisitions. It has a formula for making the transition as smooth as possible, including a policy of not firing any employee from the acquisition company for several months.
To "Amazon"	To easily purchase the book or other product you want, using trustworthy information, and being confident it'll be delivered on time, anywhere you want it to go.	Amazon built one of the most successful early Net-only brands by offering immediate availability of a broad inventory and extraordinary customer support and ease of ordering.
To "Dell"	To integrate all aspects of a customer-direct experience and service what you sell better than anyone else.	As noted, Dell has used its direct-to-customer business model to make sure that the customer experience is as important and highly valued as its product.
To "Nordstrom"	To be there for the customer without question.	Nordstrom's extraordinary customer service and policy of accepting all customer returns helped raise the bar for customer service in the retailing industry.

and even a product advantage alone are not enough to survive in the Net Future.

When thinking the Max-e-Marketing way, management will look at providing value within the full-circle relationship the company has with its customers. Without such a point of view, a company is indeed at the mercy of commodifiers. With it, verb branding can be a powerful word-of-mouth brand builder and a constant reminder of innovation and leadership.

HOW TO MARKET PROCESS AS PRODUCT

Marketing the process means making greater use of the customer as company evangelist. Creating marketing programs aimed at stimulating word of mouth is vital in the Net Future. Not only is it easier to do in a wired world than ever before but also those customer-evangelists have greater credibility than traditional advertising. Word-of-mouth advertising can help circumvent the problems discussed earlier of marketing to a media-weary public.

In the Net Future, as the process more and more becomes the message, it becomes possible to provide each customer with a uniquely satisfying experience. Companies must call attention to that experience as the keystone of their traditional marketing efforts. Advertising, public relations, direct mail programs—all must ensure that customers hear about the benefits of a true customer care focus and see its value. And, when Max-e-Marketers "make everything they do add to what they know," they want to build a direct response element into every brand-building message.

Authenticity is a powerful sales message, and an authentic, positive brand experience—or hearing about one—is the most powerful sales rep of all.

When interactive brand experience becomes a priority, it extends beyond the sale to create a continuing relationship that truly unlocks the potential of each customer. This is the subject discussed in the next Max-e-Marketing imperative: "Factor Future Value into Every Move You Make. "

NOTES

1. The following is based on the authors' interviews with Bill Bass, Senior Vice President E-Commerce at Lands' End.
2. The following is based on the authors' interview with Anne Busquet, President of Interactive Services and New Business at American Express.
3. Based on the authors' interview with Tina Guegold, Director of Corporate Marketing at Symix.

Factor Future Value into Every Move You Make

Make the Brand Experience Exceed the Brand Perception

Marketers are being confronted by customers whose expectations about how and when a company is accessible to them have been dramatically reset by the Internet. On the one hand, access to helpful information before and after the sale must now be available when, where, and how the customer wants. On the other hand, real-time, on-demand availability is new for most companies.

As we move further into the Net Future, this information explosion will have a profound effect on end-user and business customer attitudes, not only in e-commerce, but in the bricks-and-mortar world as well.

When it comes to direct customer interaction, more often than not, the majority of companies still treat it as an afterthought and, at worst, as a nuisance. It is seen as an expense rather than an investment in the value of the business.

Yet, to satisfy and retain the loyalty of the Net Future customer, companies must provide a complete and pleasurable end-to-end experience. This is true whether the sale is made to a car buyer in a showroom or by someone visiting a mall or clicking through a cybershop or by a manufacturer's representative selling to another business. Repeat sales are dependent on both product satisfaction and the interactive relationship that follows the sale.

It has been commonplace for years in the business world to hear talk about being customer-centric. It's easy to talk the talk, but few companies actually walk the walk. What is surprising, given the one-to-one relationships that new technologies can much more easily and inexpensively create, is the state of the customer experience on the Net.

One survey demonstrated that customer-service levels online still have a long way to go. It showed that before a sale, 56 percent of online customer requests are resolved immediately. After the sale, the percentage drops dramatically to 17 percent.[1]

The sad fact of life in the early years of the new millennium is that most companies are moving into the Net Future with product-focused marketing managers leading the charge. Simply saying in a marketing plan that a company is customer-focused is very different from genuinely caring about the customer's experience. And the customer soon discovers the difference.

The good news is that, with customer dissatisfaction the rule rather than the exception, failed expectations can be turned into a competitive advantage if a company understands what it needs to do differently in listening to and then delighting the customer.

THE WEB-CENTRIC CUSTOMER EXPERIENCE

Make no mistake: it is the environment of the Web that increasingly will drive customer expectations. A survey of 2600 senior executives throughout the United States recently found that currently, 66 percent of the time customers make contact via the telephone.[2] Only 23 percent of the time was it done by e-mail or through the company Web site. Those same executives predict that 2 years from now their companies will have made the shift to digital customer management via e-mail or at their Web site. This will drop telephone communication down to only 25 percent of all contacts from customers. (See Table 6.1.[3])

In addition, only 17 percent of the executives surveyed reported total contact integration among all the various customer touch points. And only 54 percent expected to achieve that total integration within 2 years.

This has important implications for mastering the art of making Web-based interaction a great brand experience. If you don't get it right, the bulk of the customer experience could potentially be worse than it is right now despite the advantages offered by interactivity.

The Net Future shift to digital contact has already taken place at Fidelity Investments.[4] For every 50,000 telephone interactions between Fidelity and its customers, there are 400,000 Web interactions. In addition, when someone is given a choice between talking to a representative on the telephone or using interactive digital communication via the Net, only 9 percent of people elect to talk on the phone.

Table 6.1 How Customers Make Contact

	Primary Method Today (%)	Primary Method in 2 Years (%)
Phone	66.2	24.6
E-mail	19.6	42.3
Web site	3.5	28.1
At our physical location	6.9	3.1
Mail	3.8	1.9

Source: Net Future Institute research.

THE CHANGING MIND-SET OF THE NEW INTERNET-SAVVY CONSUMER

The business world is wired with intranets that support streamlined communication between the company and its employees as well as between employees with one another. So, it's natural for someone at home to ask: "If I can send one e-mail at work and have it automatically reach all the appropriate parties with the touch of a key, then why can't my experience outside the office satisfy my needs as easily?"

And for the savvy consumer to think: "If these people can spend tens and hundreds of millions of dollars bombarding me with messages about how wonderful that product or service can be, why can't someone there look after me properly after I buy the stuff and want some help?"

As more people in their jobs become used to having advanced information technology at their fingertips, that experience translates into new expectations at home any time that person contacts a company to fulfill a personal request.

In the United States, where more than 50 million people are connected to the Internet, anyone can plug into the buzz about a company's product at any time from anywhere. Perception is constantly colliding with Web "e-pinions" and the reality of what competitors are saying is just a click away. In the Net Future, there are voices always out there ready to counter an investment in creating an attractive perception of a brand in the consumer's mind. And as more people get connected everywhere in the world, the challenge will only increase.

This is the time when the brand experience—how a company interacts directly with the end user and with its business customers—must counter the 24/7 noise that affects the perception of the brand. What matters most is the responsive, individual dialogue you build with the customer. In the end, it's the special relationship you control that must weather the storm.

WHAT YOU DO TO, WITH, AND FOR THE CUSTOMER

The billion dollar questions in the Net Future center on understanding the present value of all the interactions a company has with its customers and which relationship drivers are critical in leveraging future value. With the accelerating pace of change an overwhelming reality, every move a company makes must focus on what will be as well as on what is. It is time for any company that wants to survive and prosper in this new world to answer these three questions:

1. What is the present value of the relationship with its customers?

2. What is its Relationship Effectiveness Quotient compared to competitors?

3. What are the relationship drivers creating future value in the category?

At McCann Relationship Marketing (MRM), in order to assist clients such as Microsoft, Sprint, and Sirius, in finding the right answers, the agency developed a proprietary business solution tool called the Future Value Model™. It is based on the premise that the future value of the enterprise grows out of the sum of the brand value and the relationship value—the aggregate contribution of all future customer interactions.

Rather than the traditional marketing focus on lifetime value of an individual customer, this approach begins by focusing on the overall value of the customer relationship itself. It incorporates accepted accounting practices to come up with a reliable and credible financial valuation. In addition to the Relationship Valuation module, it includes a Competitive Ranking module and an Analysis of Relationship Drivers module to identify opportunities. The outcome is a future value growth strategy.

The concept of setting a value on the relationship just as you might set a value on the company's brand is entirely new to most companies. What works so well about it is that it creates a yardstick for measuring future Max-e-Marketing effectiveness and for allocating adequate budgets focused on the most promising leverage points.

In a business world where change is the only constant, the Future Value Model keeps one foot in the present while bringing the full weight of the marketing process into capitalizing on what is coming next.

The result is a shift from focusing on Customer Relationship Management to focusing on Customer Value Management. (See Table 6.2.)

What you do to, with, and for the customer to strengthen the relationship becomes a primary force in shaping future value and brand equity.

A CHECKLIST FOR BUILDING FUTURE VALUE: RESPONDING *TO* THE CUSTOMER

This set of drivers looks at how you are interacting with prospects and customers online and offline and at the many ways you can use what you know about prospects and customers to cross-sell, upsell, friend-sell (referrals), and new-sell (introduce new offerings) so as to maximize sales and profits.

- *Do you involve customers in the product and service planning process?*

The immediacy of the Internet and the ease of conducting target audience surveys in real-time opens up an invaluable new resource for product-planning initiatives not readily available before.

- *Do you provide a choice of response methods and allow the customer to choose?*

Customers will want to be able to contact you at their convenience, not yours. That means not only being available in multiple ways but also making sure that those different contact points are prepared to interact appropriately.

- *Do you make products and services readily available and offer hassle-free ordering?*

Table 6.2 Relationship Value Drivers

WHAT YOU DO

What You Do *to* the Customer	What You Do *with* the Customer	What You Do *for* the Customer
• Respond to	• Inform/educate with	• Extra value for
• Bring product benefits to	• Interact with	• Recognition for
• Bring service benefits to	• Join with	• Customize for

FUTURE VALUE ACTIVATORS

• Prompt, courteous, informative contact	• Complaint handling	• Frequent buyer rewards
• Listen and learn	• Help lines	• Exclusive offers
• Protect privacy	• Web chat	• Loyalty recognition
• Cross-sell	• Clubs	• One-of-a-kind products
• Friend-sell	• Events	• Guaranteed satisfaction
• Upsell	• Seminars	• Remember past behavior
• New sell	• Custom publications	• Personalized service

The ubiquity of the Net means you, as a marketer, must be ubiquitous too. In the new environment, there are a thousand paths to your Web site and unlimited potential connections you can make to other home pages. Your products must not only be available, but they must be available when and wherever your customers might look for them.

- *Do you encourage repeat sales (cross-sell, upsell, friend-sell, new sell)?*

Prudential.com brings together in one place for the first time its various businesses.

You can get insurance quotes, prices, and other useful info from Prudential insurance. You can manage your money online, take out a home equity loan, pay bills, and make other financial transactions with Prudential, the banker. You can browse through listings of homes all across North America offered by Prudential Real Estate. It's a cross-selling paradise for Prudential Marketing Services. And, the Internet opens up a whole new world of upselling (see American Express' Green-Gold-Platinum upsell online), friend-selling rewards (see AOL's $50 offer), and a great platform for selling your new products and services (see Microsoft MSN).

- *Do you create future value from your existing customer base?*

One of the easiest ways to lose market share in the Net Future will be to fail to take advantage of what you know about each customer to generate the maximum amount of revenue using the relevant relationship drivers over time.

- *Do you respect the privacy of the information provided by your customers?*

An unequivocal commitment to protecting privacy, clearly stating your Web site privacy policy and living up to every word of it, is essential to retaining the trust of your customers. Abuse or lose customer confidence and you've lost everything.

Factor the relationship drivers and the relationship activators into every move you make. With each customer contact, you need to ask yourself:

- What are all the ways I can listen to and learn from this customer?

- What are all the added-value benefits I can sell to this customer?

- What are all the ways I can get this customer to attract new customers?

A CHECKLIST FOR BUILDING FUTURE VALUE: WORKING *WITH* THE CUSTOMER

This set of drivers centers around increased involvement and productive interaction. It provides the focal point for marketing programs that result in community building and in deepening the relationship between the brand and the customer.

Do you inform and educate the customer?

- Do you provide in an easily understood and accessible way all the information needed for the customer to enjoy using your product or service?

- Do you rely upon your customer feedback to determine what aspects need additional information and education?

- Do you go to extremes to relieve the customer of worries or concerns? Zane's Cycles, a speciality bike shop in Branford, Connecticut, which is battling to survive against a nearby sports superstore, partners with UPS so that it can send an e-mail giving shipping details and arrival date the moment a bike is shipped.

- Do you provide the educational information your target market wants without making the brand intrusive? Visit MixingSpoon.com to see how GE Appliances does it. You'll find helpfull cooking solutions complete with nutritional information for today's busy families—and barely a mention of GE as the sponsor.

Do you interact with the customer in meaningful ways?

- Do you take lessons from Amazon, e-Bay, AOL, and the other masters of Web content? Amazon's Purchase Circles, Gift Registry, One-Click Purchase, and other innovations are a model of how to interact with Web travelers by the tens of millions in a personal, warm, and helpful way that keeps them coming back for more.

- Do you have substantive, convenient, and fast methods for collecting and acting upon customer complaints? Consider a complaint to be one of the best things that can happen. Research has shown again and again that quick response to an individual's complaint is the route to winning a long-time repeat customer.

Some estimates suggest that more than half of dissatisfied customers don't bother to complain. They just say good-bye to the offending company. If you need help with complaints, you may want to talk to the folks at ugetheard.com.

The site provides a mechanism for customers to lodge complaints with responsible representatives of more than 3000 companies.

- Do you connect with customers signing up to join a club or participating at an event you sponsor?
- Do you invite membership in a continuing relationship with special benefits tied to a long-term commitment?
- Do you offer incentives to encourage visitors to register at your Web site?
- Do you offer educational seminars or a custom publication that encourages customer participation?

A CHECKLIST FOR BUILDING FUTURE VALUE: WHAT YOU DO *FOR* THE CUSTOMER

This set of drivers is the ultimate step creating a unique bond to differentiate the business from the competition. This is where you have the best opportunity to forge a lasting relationship with your most valued customers.

Do you offer a mind-boggling Extra Value Proposition?

American Express Platinum cardholders can take a companion along free on an international flight—yes, even in first class. British Airways totally redesigned the first class cabin to provide a private dining, sleeping, and work space for each of its most desirable passengers, and then became the first airline to offer Business Class travelers a fully reclining seat for cross-Atlantic travel.

Do you tier customers according to sales revenue and scale benefits at corresponding levels of contribution to the bottom line?

Airline frequent-flyer programs wrote the book on this one.

Do you provide an absolute satisfaction guarantee and make good on it?
Do you call attention to the offer at every opportunity?

Lands' End, the casual clothing catalog company, built a very successful business around the simplest and most powerful message any company can send. One word tells it all: *guaranteed*. Period.

Do you acknowledge customers who return to you after trying out the competition?

Saying "thank you" can work wonders.

Do you create one-of-a-kind products that shut out the competition forever?

You can build your own customized Nike athletic shoe at NikeID.com and then put any brand name you want on it. You can customize the style of Levi's Original Spin jeans and get a perfect fit every time. You can order a Barbie Doll with the hair color and outfit chosen by you. Technology's next business miracle, mass customization, is beginning to pick up steam. You can read more about it in Imperative 4.

Do you continually innovate pleasant surprises for your best customers?

Saks department store surprises its premium charge cardholders with skipped payment months prior to Christmas and invites them to special cocktail receptions offering exclusive seasonal previews.

Do you offer personalized service that remembers past behavior and preferences?

The Four Seasons and Ritz Carlton hotel chains pioneered remembering whether its preferred guests prefer a "soft" or a "firm" pillow, a quiet room, or a particular nightcap. Everything is waiting just for you upon check-in.

HOW KITCHENAID DELIVERS EXTRA VALUE TO THE CUSTOMER

KitchenAid has a brand that dates back to 1919, when it launched the stand mixer that is still its signature product. The KitchenAid mixer is such an American icon that the silhouette of the cantilevered motor hanging over a bowl is one of the few product shapes that is trademarked.

The company recently realized that, in a global environment that was rapidly commoditizing the sale of small appliances, it needed to reorganize itself around relationships rather than product function to take advantage of the goodwill that KitchenAid had built with its customers over the years.

That relationship equity was built by focusing on what customers really want and empowering customer service representatives to be certain that each customer's total experience with the company exceeds expectations. For example, in one instance, a customer whose 8-year-old blender wouldn't start contacted the company about it. Instead of repairing the appliance, KitchenAid sent the man a new blender.

Brian Maynard, Brand Director, Integrated Marketing, views collecting and using information from customers as central to the total customer experience. Maynard is a proponent of both of the Max-e-Marketing imperatives: "Use what you know to drive what you do." and "Make the brand experience exceed brand expectations."[5] Maynard says:

> "One of the reasons we participate in probably 200 bridal events a year—trade shows and events sponsored by retailers, magazines, and others—is because we know from our customer data that there is a progression in our customers' relationship with us. They tend to start with small appliances, such as a stand mixer, and then move to larger appliances such as refrigerators. Our research has shown that if someone buys one appliance from us, they are extremely likely to buy a second one. If they own two, they are dramatically more likely to buy a third.
>
> "When someone calls with a problem, the customer service rep has access to the database with the customer's entire history with KitchenAid. It includes data on any product they have ever bought from us. One of the most important functions of our customer service approach is getting information that can help us do things better and finding ways to wow the customer.
>
> "An example of wowing the customer is our total replacement warranty. It also enables us to gather

information and helps to improve our products and maintain a very low replacement rate."

HAVING THE PEOPLE WHO MAKE THE STUFF TALK WITH THE PEOPLE WHO BUY THE STUFF

Maynard tells us that, in many cases, the person who answers the phone at KitchenAid is someone who was working on building the product that morning.

"We have a program where the people who work in manufacturing can spend 4 hours on the assembly line and 4 hours talking with customers when they call the help line. Customers are amazed that they can actually talk with someone who is involved in making the product they bought from KitchenAid.

"Our customers tell us they have come to rely on us for the right advice. So sometimes we get questions like, "Why can't I get my bread to rise?" Being there with the right answer becomes as much a part of our brand equity as anything else we do in manufacturing or distribution.

"Our products are quite expensive; a KitchenAid appliance costs two to four times those of our next closest competitor. You can't get away with charging more without a good brand experience, and you can't have a good brand experience without constant feedback and a commitment to constantly finding ways to improve the experience."

Any marketer in the new Net economy can benefit from studying the established KitchenAid policies.

With its twentieth-century customer service heritage, it was a simple step for KitchenAid to move on to the Internet and add new dimensions to what it is doing to, for, and with its customers.

CAREWARE FOR CUSTOMER CARE

Customer care is a cornerstone of the Max-e-Marketing approach to creating future value. But there is a downside. It can also be a major cost center. Behind the scene, taking care of customers in the e-economy is driven by an array of high-tech tools that can make the high-touch experience affordable and practical.

The good news is the emergence of "careware," the customer-care software, and companies that can manage almost every aspect of the caring process for you.

Companies can "do as little as possible," as discussed in Imperative 4, while still reaping the benefits of providing world-class customer service.

A group of intermediaries has sprung up to automate every facet of Relationship Marketing, from completion of membership forms at a Web site to running a reward program, sending targeted e-mails, disturbing samples, and even providing a representative to communicate with customers in your name online and offline.

It is much more than outsourcing in the usual sense of the word. As noted in Imperative 4, we call it "team sourcing" because a company is, in effect, partnering with a team of experts that seamlessly provides the customer care vital to building the relationship brand—and that is in a position to do it more effectively and efficiently. Careware providers represent an expanding Web-enabled customer interaction resource estimated at more than $20 billion.[6]

One might wonder if automating customer contact could reduce the potential for the kind of human interaction that often solidifies a company's connection with its own customers. It might.

But most "careware" companies are not in the business of eliminating human connection. Automated software in the Net economy is the underlying technology that oils the wheels of a person-to-person contact machine. It opens up additional channels of communication and integrates them with a human interface at less cost.

The goal is to use costly human labor more efficiently. If it takes a person a week to respond to a deluge of e-mail, compared to an automated real-time system that can give an immediate answer and refer the query to a human when it makes sense, the immediacy may be more important than providing a more detailed answer later to a time-pressured customer.

"Customer service is reactive," says Richard Hebert, President and CEO of iSKY, which provides multichannel customer support for many *Fortune 500* companies.[7] "Customer care is different. It's very strategic, linking together a unique set of customer service functions to create a presumptive customer relationship." Says Hebert:

> "We put a concierge bell icon on our client's Web site for the various communications channels: telephone, voice over IP (Internet protocol), text chat, e-mail, fax, and video. We have found the telephone is still the best channel for immediacy, for the ability to comprehend and impart tone and emotion.

"Even when we're providing customer support for a pure e-commerce company, more than half the time the customer chooses to interact telephonically. Maybe that's a function of our customer base, but it's a pretty broad base. Aggregate numbers show 85 percent of current customer contact via telephone and 15 percent interactive, up from zero a year ago. What's the most frequent customer response when asked how do you want to communicate? Telephone, e-mail, text chat, fax, voice over IP, and video, in that order.

"Our reps can get very involved with a customer. On a client's Web site, we can take control of your browser and push pages to you. If you're having trouble with an order form, we can fill out the form for you. If you push a help button on a Web site, it will escalate into our center and our technology will tell our rep where you've been on the site. We use triggers: if she's stuck on a certain page, we send help in the form of a pop-up assist. What we're really doing is making certain that the customer is going to have a good experience."

How is the client kept in the loop? "We provide weekly and monthly reports," says Hebert.

"Some of our clients make changes the next day, based on those findings. We can routinely differentiate top-tier customers for our clients and provide them prioritized queuing, prioritized e-mail response, and special consideration with every interaction. Special considerations range from an apology if our client did less than expected, to 5 percent off the next purchase, to providing high-value customers with a dedicated personal shopping assistant by name and extension, and advance preview of new products."

With the increasing importance of the Web as a primary mode of customer contact, there are five categories of Careware that are changing the very nature of the customer experience.

New breakthroughs are taking place that transfer the familiar potential pitfalls of customer interaction into powerful drivers of a new kind of brand experience that often exceeds the brand perception.

THE NEW KIND OF TELESERVICES

Call centers are not just the first destination of dissatisfied customers. They also are a touch point for prospective buyers who want information to help them make a buying decision. E-tailers have discovered that online customers often abandon a purchase without following through because they have a question that cannot be answered immediately. The cost of those lost sales are one reason companies have begun to integrate call centers with online commerce, allowing a customer at a company's Web site to connect instantly with a company representative by clicking one button.

Yet, call centers staffed with professional customer representatives cost an average of $6 per call in the United States.[8] They have traditionally been extremely labor-intensive; with the rise of telecommunicating as the number 1 method of communication with the customer, the number of representatives running the phones has soared. And it isn't only the United States. By the end of 2000, 1.3 million people throughout Europe are expected to work for call centers—about 1 percent of the continent's population.[9]

One factor driving the need for so many customer service representatives is that a telephone operator typically can work with only one customer at a time. The challenge is to get a handle on those costs and yet provide superior customer service. The answer is automation of the process while retaining the human element in providing superior customer service.

Live Person, whose 700 clients include American Express, QVC, and Intuit, has developed automation careware that enables interaction via live chat on the Web. Instead of being able to listen to only one caller at a time, a representative using live chat can work with four clients at once. While one caller types in a question, the rep can respond to another. It's an interactive exchange with a "live person." Rather than listening to a canned recording while waiting on hold for a service representative who "will be with you shortly," the customer gets immediate, real-time interaction.

Such Web-based services can reduce the cost of a customer service "call" to under a dollar, according to Live Person CEO Rob LoCasio. They also can transform reps into salespeople. The ability to give pertinent information to customers in real time can make a buyer of someone who might otherwise have abandoned a purchase for lack of information. Live Person says Web-based teleservices can convert 35 percent of inquiries into sales, a vast improvement over the reported 2 percent average. In some cases, customer service centers can generate substantial revenues in the course of customer dialogue.

The Web-based interaction isn't limited to online shoppers. As Internet-enabled mobile devices become more widespread, a customer who spots a product in a store but can't find a salesperson—not unusual in an era of big-box retailers—will be able to hop on a PDA, contact the company's call center, and get questions answered by a representative a thousand miles away.

THOMAS COOK'S NEW IN-HOUSE TELESERVICES SOLUTION

Thomas Cook Holdings, the venerable London-based company founded in 1854, is well known for its global currency conversion business, with kiosks located conspic-uously in airports throughout the world. The company also has a huge vacation package business. The company has 20,000 employees and 1800 locations in more than 25 countries.

With more than 20 million customers a year, Thomas Cook found itself faced with whether and how to modify its existing business to meet changing customer expectations as more customers went online.

When the company looked at how to determine moving into the Net Future environment, it decided to start what is essentially a new call-center operation that could start from scratch to create all the interactive processes and state-of-the art technologies without legacy issues.

The company established a separate unit under Thomascook.com, with a charter to help redefine how the organization would deal with its new wired consumers. Tapped to lead the effort was Paul de Laat, Customer Service and Retention Director at Thomascook.com.[10]

"We're looking at seamless customer service across all channels. We used technology from

E.piphany to help build our analytical tools to personalize every contact with each customer. Our call center technology allows us to recognize phone numbers of individuals so that on the second call we bring up the customer details on a computer screen. We have 1500 people in all our call centers, but set up a specific team for Thomascook.com, with 40 people.

"We've trained them to handle outbound e-mails as well as contacts from the Web site. We needed to build multiskilled teams, since the existing call center staff was focused only on phone and was volume-driven. We're now focused on service, not just volume.

"We look at the customer lifetime value. With millions of regular customers in our bricks network, we have access to valuable travel data. We used that data to see what products our customers buy and then determined the key characteristics, such as having children or not, that determine travel potential. We determined the basics, such as whether they travel more than twice a year. Then we looked at customer preferences, such as whether they like a certain vacation type. Then we fine-tuned the future value of that customer.

"We look at each value across each customer and look at what would happen if we got full share of that customer's wallet across this customer. This gives us the potential of this customer. This gets the focus away from the margins on a specific transaction.

"In the 'bricks' business we were not used to looking at it this way. We had to build this from scratch anyway, and we have full control of our call center. We have a separate team for the bricks business of Thomas Cook and our team of 40 has become the breeding ground for new developments. When people research their travel on our Web site and then ask us to contact them, the call will link to the real-time database. Roughly 2 percent of people at our travel site request a call back but we have a significant conversion ratio.

"We're now focusing on making our content more relevant to individuals because that's the key to increasing call requests and conversions. Our search engine on our site is a key component, because customers request exactly what they are looking for. A lot of people have been talking about this kind of customer future-value modeling, but we're actually doing it."

Whether you "team-source" your customer care call center or develop your own new set of "careware" solutions as Thomas Cook has done, you can say good-bye to the old boiler room image of telemarketing. A new day has arrived that adds value to the customer while increasing the value of the customer to you.

Most models of forecasting "lifetime customer value" focus solely on the value of the individual customer. However, to truly assess future value of customer assets, a company must look at the aggregated value of its entire database, including the future value of information customers provide that can be used to develop new products and businesses and to open up new strategic possibilities.

THE NEW KIND OF DIRECT MAIL: E-MAIL

Traditional direct mail still has its unique multidimensional targeting role to play! But it now has a potent new electronic aspect. We first talked about permission-based e-mail systems in Imperative 3. With e-mail, the marketer has an extraordinarily low-cost, real-time resource for providing exceptional customer service that can lead to increased sales and strengthened relationships. Using e-mail, you can integrate online information with an offline database to anticipate and respond to customer needs even before the customer recognizes them.

For example, it is now possible to forecast future customer behavior based on how he or she explores a Web site. The information-gathering process may not require a customer to register or log in; indeed, it may not even require a purchase. Based on what a customer clicks on and how much time is spent on a given page, e-mails can be generated that focus on items or services that are most likely to match observed interests. The same technology can also be used to make the next visit serve up individualized Web pages.

The ability to instantaneously personalize appropriate messages is one of the most dramatic attributes of Web marketing. Like traditional direct mail, it is addressable and accountable; the big difference, of course, is that it is so much more affordable.

UserTrends is one of the companies that makes personalized e-mail possible. CEO Bruce Eisen calls it "CRM without turning people off."[11] The company tracks users through a specific Web site and learns a person's potential interests based on what they look at. The data captured is used in real time to target e-mails sending relevant messages to each individual.

"Marketing personnel are starting to understand what they can do with this technology," says Eisen.

"E-mail marketing is growing very quickly. In a typical mail campaign, it might cost 75 cents for each response, though costs can vary. When targeted with e-mail, that can be down to 11 to 14 cents."

Using real-time data also allows marketers to get comprehensive progress reports on response rates while a campaign is still in progress and quickly change direction if necessary. UserTrends has found that broad-based e-mail campaigns garner anywhere from 6 to 12 percent response rates, while carefully targeted e-mail campaigns receive anywhere from 18 to 50 percent response.

THE NEW KIND OF CUSTOMER REWARD PROGRAMS

One way to build relationships is to reward customers for their loyalty in the way they want to be rewarded. To maximize the value of those rewards, they need to be

1. Meaningful
2. Tailored to the individual
3. Easy to earn
4. Speedily awarded.

"Except for supermarkets, airlines, and credit cards, individual retailers cannot afford sufficient reward value given their share of wallet. Consumers don't shop at any one store; they shop at a selected network of retailers," says West Shell III, Chairman and CEO of Netcentives.[12]

The company partners with retailers and other companies to offer online rewards programs that award points for browsing, buying, or receiving e-mail. Consumers can then use the points to get merchandise, travel, or other benefits.

The real power of such programs lies in a company's ability to expand the number of places where a consumer can earn and spend points. That means that a company must now reward customers for being loyal not just to that company but to the network of partners it has built up around itself. Encouraging loyalty to other companies is a distinctly new marketing twist to traditional customer rewards programs.

Companies are also learning to integrate online and offline rewards programs. People who buy $100 worth of clothes at The Gap can not only earn frequent-flyer miles on United or Delta. If they register one of their credit cards with Netcentives and use it for their Gap purchase, they will also get an e-mail thanking them for buying and letting them know how many frequent-flyer miles have been added to their account. The thank you also serves as an opportunity to resell, upsell, or cross-sell.

In addition, Netcentives receives information from 90 percent of the credit cards in the United States, so the miles added also can show up on their credit card statement.

Integrating online and offline loyalty programs over time allows companies to learn which messages were most successful at changing actual buying behavior, not just of groups but *customer by customer*.

"As people interact with our customers, that behavior starts showing up in their databases. We can track whether an inactive consumer responds to a particular message and/or incentive," says Shell.

The ability for permission-based programs to track individual behavior enables highly targeted messages and promotional strategies.

For example, a company can target an inactive buyer with a message aimed at simply getting him or her into the store. A more active buyer can be targeted with a message designed to up the average purchase amount per store visit.

"Loyalty is a participation sport. You need to have continuous, relevant interaction between the customer and company over time to build trust and develop meaningful relationship value," says Shell.

THE NEW KIND OF HELP LINE

E-mail may be one way to cut the cost of communicating with customers, but it's a double-edged sword. In the early days of the Internet, companies that got excited about the possibilities for customer feedback soon found themselves with too much of a good thing. They were overwhelmed by the sheer volume of e-mail requests, demands, comments, and complaints. The automated help line is one solution.

A company can automate its process of deciding how help line e-mails get answered. Initial screening can be done using a combination of artificial intelligence and natural language recognition to automate the process for interaction in real time. The customer who types in a question can receive a response that appears to be generated by a person when, in fact, it is a computer analyzing the query and determining whether it needs to ask the customer for more information or pull a response from a database.

Automated analysis also can determine whether the customer's inquiry needs to be referred to a human being, and route the inquiry to a call center representative.

Tesco, the United Kingdom's largest supermarket chain and one of the world's smartest relationship marketers, uses systems such as Brightware Concierge to handle the automation of customer service. Tesco Direct, the company's online branch, has seen a 300 percent increase in call center productivity, measured in terms of the number of customer interactions per day and average response time, since adopting the automated screening.[13]

THE NEW VOICE OF THE CUSTOMER

Because it makes interaction so affordable, the Internet enables consumers to help drive product development, improve services, and prevent marketing problems before they arise. In the Digital Age, even smaller companies with insignificant marketing budgets can still use the Net to conduct highly cost-effective sampling, opinion testing, and test marketing. By conducting online surveys and tapping into established online focus groups, you can do the kind of effective market research that previously required large budgets and lots of time.

Anyone who has ever run a focus group knows what it takes to recruit the appropriate participants, set up a time and place where they can gather, conduct the sessions professionally, and transcribe and analyze the results. Online focus groups, on the other hand, can streamline the recruitment process, provide a more global cross-section of participants, and give instantaneous feedback.

NFO, a leader in market research for more than half a century recently acquired by Interpublic Group of Companies (IPG), has assembled a team of 450,000 online panelists to eliminate many of the delays that once hampered research.[14] Collectively called NetSource, the panelists are recruited from a wide variety of online and offline communities. A client company can use NetSource or provide its own panelists.

Participants doing product testing are asked to try the products for a couple of weeks. Then, on a specific date, they log on and join the online discussion. Much like offline focus groups, all participants can see the text of what everyone else is saying, including the moderator, but can't see the client's comments to the moderator.

There are some disadvantages associated with the business of conducting research on the Web. For one thing, there are entire demographic populations that are not yet adequately represented by online sampling. Studies for the American Association of Retired People (AARP), for example, are still best conducted offline, says Ann Green, NFO's Vice President of E-Commerce and Retail.

Also, because the researchers cannot see respondents' facial expressions or body language, they have no way of gauging their mood or the tone of their answers. Of course, online responses tend to be more candid because the respondent sees himself or herself as anonymous. The other downside is that it is not always as easy to spot the one oddball who seems to show up at each in-person focus group session.

The dynamic is the reverse of what happens in an offline group, Green says; online responses are more accurate than those given offline. NFO can tackle this problem by using their prescreened panel to supplement an initial trial evaluation and subsequent in-person discussions. Another way to ensure more accurate results is to have online focus groups that are as large as possible (several thousand are not uncommon), and make sure the moderator is a master of online communication.

WHAT WILL BE CAN COUNT FOR MORE THAN WHAT IS

All this personal attention comes at a cost. Collectibles.com, the online operation of Shop At Home Inc., spent $15 million on integrating and revamping its Web site, call center, databases, and hardware to be able to target the content of its Web site more closely to what customers are already interested in learning.

However, results can be impressive. In the case of Shop At Home, the margin on its revenues was 38 percent. But even without such dramatic results, building a trusted Relationship Brand is a core business need in Max-e-Marketing in the Net Future:

Every move a company makes must be aimed at building the future aggregate value of its customers because that value determines the future value of the company.

Max-e-Marketing success is driven by how well any company forges a direct relationship with its customers. That connection involves the all-important marketing components of the Net Future. You can now address accessible customers in an accountable and affordable manner with increased accountability. What you do to, with, and for your customers using the four A's becomes the set of drivers that unleash customer potential and future value.

Why is future value so important? Because any company that does not stay focused on the future while doing what must be done to stay viable in the present is doomed to failure in a rapidly changing economy.

The future we now face has a nasty way of arriving sooner than almost anyone anticipates. Three-year planning used to be a business standard; now three-month planning is the norm at the smartest companies.

At your company, you must constantly be asking, "What marketing trends are likely to reshape this category in the next 18 months? How will these changes impact the relationship with our customers? How will they change what we must do to, with, and for the customer to enhance the brand experience? What can we do today to build future value tomorrow?"

But keeping an eye on the future means keeping up with the new marketing technologies that will shape that future. How do you organize internally to ally Marketing and IT so as to enable the best future outcome. For the answer, turn to the seventh and final imperative, which focuses on forming a new partnership between the IT professionals and the Relationship Marketing professionals.

NOTES

1. Based on a Harris Interactive survey of 509 Internet consumers.
2. Based on a Net Future Institute survey, conducted in 2000, of 2600 senior executives throughout the United States.
3. Based on a Net Future Institute survey, conducted in 2000, of 2600 senior executives throughout the United States.
4. The following is based on the authors' interview with Steve Elterich, President of Fidelity E-Business.
5. Based on the authors' interview with Brian Maynard, Brand Director, Integrated Marketing of KitchenAid.
6. Based on the authors' interview with Rob LoCasio, President and CEO, Live Person.

7. Based on the authors' interview with Richard Hebert, President and CEO of iSKY.
8. The information in this section about teleservices is based on the authors' interview with Rob LoCasio, President and CEO, Live Person.
9. Taken from a research study conducted by Datamonitor, London, 1999.
10. The following is based on the authors' interview with Paul de Laat, Customer Service and Retention Director at Thomascook.com.
11. Based on the authors' interview with Bruce Eisen, CEO of UserTrends.
12. Based on the authors' interview with West Shell, Chairman and CEO of Netcentives.
13. Based on the authors' interview with Chuck Williams, CEO of BrightWare.
14. Based on the authors' interview with Ann Green, Vice President of E-Commerce and Retail at NFO.

Make Business Responsible for Marketing and Marketing Responsible for Business

Form a New Partnership Between IT and Marketing

Marketing, in the Net economy, becomes the core of an organization's future. Simple to say, hard to do.

How do you gear up internally? Who should be in charge? What is the actual role of marketing in an inter-connected real-time world, where the customer is totally empowered? How does a company move fast enough to keep up with changing customer expectations? Where does IT and Marketing come together?

How a company answers these questions may mean the difference between success and failure in efforts to implement the other six imperatives of Max-e-Marketing.

In many ways, this is the toughest part: getting everything *inside* a company lined up properly to serve customers *outside* that company. To be successful in this new world, companies will have to be realigned internally, with new partnerships and innovative leadership.

To take just one example, implementing the 51 percent rule—that says at least 51 percent of all communications circulated throughout the organization should originate from external sources—may require a fundamental shift in the way information flows into and throughout a company. It may require a reorganization of the Information Technology (IT) group, a rethinking of who is responsible for communications within the company, and what type of communications are missing.

Perhaps most important to the optimization of marketing results discussed throughout this book is how to get all the new ways of doing business to coincide with all the ways business was conducted before the Digital Age.

Established companies have become the new pacesetters on the Net, as many eager start-ups see hope turn to despair. In one survey of business executives, how to integrate traditional methods of doing business with their online efforts rated as the top issue. (See Table 7.1.)

It is interesting to note that the research shows that this integration of the traditional and the new is not expected to get any easier in the next few years. The cultural changes necessary to mesh online and offline strategies are substantial, and this is expected to continue to be a primary concern of senior executives for the foreseeable future.

Frequently, companies who were quick to perceive the possibilities of the Net acted quickly to institute separate e-commerce divisions. Many of these early movers now

Table 7.1 Integrating Traditional and Online Methods of Doing Business

Which matters most in the Net Future?
1. Successful ways to integrate online and offline business strategies
2. Working collaboratively and knowledge sharing
3. The use of experience communities and real-time collaborative knowledge

What do you anticipate being most important 2 years from now?
1. Successful ways to integrate online and offline business strategies
2. Working collaboratively and knowledge sharing
3. The use of experience communities and real-time collaborative knowledge

Source: Net Future Institute research

find themselves realizing that e-commerce cannot be separated from other aspects of business they conduct. As a result, they are developing new organizational structures that reflect the increasing integration between their Net and non-Net activities.

FROM MARKETING DEPARTMENT TO MARKETING COMPANIES

As the digital revolution tore through the corporate landscape in the late 1990s, managers explored various approaches for getting into the e-Business game.

This revolution started with marketing departments, back in the early days—way back in 1994! Those were the pioneering days of Netscape and its browser, which gave anyone who was interested an easy way to access a rapidly expanding world of information.

As the commercial Internet evolved, the responsibility and involvement for Web interaction with customers also developed and migrated within the Enterprise, like some sort of electronic corporate nomad. This evolution took place in five stages.[1]

MARKETING DEPARTMENTS GET THE BALL ROLLING

Marketing departments were often responsible for the Brochureware stage of the Net, when companies simply transferred what they were doing in their existing communications efforts onto the Net. Since the Web first appeared as a publishing medium, those who knew how to create content-based documents—often the marketing talent within an organization—got the assignment, partly by default.

Also, the commercial Net in the early days generally wasn't considered "heavy-duty" technology by many executives, and IT departments remained focused on core operating systems for their companies.

"NEW MEDIA" AND INTERACTIVE DEPARTMENTS TAKE OVER

Interactive Divisions and New Media departments entered the scene to deal with the New Content arena, when true interactivity of the Net finally started.

Companies started to solicit e-mail responses. This was the time when people with "new media" in their title could change jobs and triple their salaries overnight. Media companies were broadly raided by Net start-ups, which desperately needed people who understood content creation and management.

Marketing departments often worked hand in hand with "New Media" mavens, many highly innovative individuals who approached the Net as truly a different animal. Some within the Enterprise viewed these "New Media" types as too different and radical to know about how to create "real" business using the Net. A number of the most daring of these people left to join Net start-ups, many becoming instant multimillionaires.

Eyebrows in IT departments also were beginning to be raised at this stage. Directors of New Media were asked about their new, online customers and how they related to the company's traditional customer set. This raised the new issue of how to reconcile the two customer sets, setting in motion the creation of new ideas and technologies to link the old and new databases.

IT TAKES OVER

IT departments finally got involved in the late 1990s, as the corporate intranet was born. Connecting workers electronically through the power of the Net's open technology looked like the saving grace for many large corporations. Finally, a way to "save" money using all this new technology!

Suddenly, workers throughout the world were given a new tool, thus providing every level of the enterprise access to a world of information—not just about the inner workings of their companies but also about the inner and outer workings of interconnected corporations throughout the world.

Ford Motor Company let its workers buy cars online at a discount, Dallas-based Baylor Health Care System's four hospitals electronically connected contract reviews, early-Intranet user Hewlett-Packard flowed information to its globally connected workforce.

The genie had escaped! Organizations began to face the issue of how to manage this new, widespread availability of knowledge and information. As more and more employees learned how to apply for jobs online, yet another issue of the Net economy came to the forefront: how to recruit and retain talent. This was the high point for Net start-ups raiding established companies for employees.

In one survey of business executives (see Table 7.2), 67 percent of executives surveyed said they would be "likely" to change jobs if faced with an "incredible Net start-up opportunity." This put even more pressure on the Enterprise to come up with innovative employee retention programs.

More corporatewide departments began to look at the implications of the Internet on their corporate culture. HR departments could automate employee benefits, legal departments could electronically share documents, and top managers started to look at productivity of their workers. The promise of increased efficiency fell onto the shoulders of heavily burdened IT departments, many of

Table 7.2 If an Incredible Net Start-Up Opportunity Came Along, How Likely Would You Be to Take It?[2]

Extremely likely	30%
Somewhat likely	37%
Somewhat unlikely	20%
Extremely unlikely	18%

Source: Net Future Institute research.

which were just beginning to figure out how to deal with the Y2K issue then on the horizon.

THE BUSINESS INTERCONNECTIONS

The profit centers of organizations got involved at this stage, capitalizing on the birth of the extranet. The extranet is basically the same as the intranet, except that it is used *outside* the Enterprise. With more companies deploying extranets, more businesses could be interconnected, allowing more information about products, supplies, and inventory to flow back and forth.

In addition, companies could finally electronically and more easily connect with customers, business suppliers, distributors, and business partners. More promises of cost savings! While IT was focusing on initial cost savings of corporate intranets, and marketing departments were seeking new revenue streams from the Web, various parts of the businesses started to do business differently using extranets. This connectivity between company and customer, company and supplier, and company and distributor ultimately led to the creation and explosion of digital e-marketplaces and the total transformation of the B-to-B marketing scene as discussed in Imperative 4.

EVERYBODY GETS INTO THE ACT

During the fifth wave, the e-Business stage, every division of a corporate entity is involved. The Internet finally gets interwoven into the fabric of companies—not to mention industries and people's habits and behaviors.

The wired organization will interact with the wired consumer, with rising customer expectations, as wired workers and wired consumers are self-retrained on how to have a mutually rewarding experience. Accountability will change, as companies become enabled to measure results against all transactions. When the customer speaks, the organization will learn how to be mobilized to respond.

Every part of the Enterprise will be called on to assist in how it is portrayed to its customers, and will be given at least part of the responsibility for each experience of each customer at every contact point with the company.

The marketing department will be heavily involved again as companies focus once more on the outward connections that result from all the reshaping of internal systems and processes designed to meet customer need.

IT and marketing managers will find themselves in more meetings with each other, as the internal workings and outward customer connections of companies become linked.

And in true Max-e-Marketing fashion, all forms of interactive communications between customer and company become integrated to meet a common strategic objective, regardless of where they originate within the organization.

BEWARE OF WEAK LINKS

In the 1980s, the personal computer made it easier and cheaper to maintain databases of customers and their interests. Direct marketing, formerly limited to selling without an intermediary, began its transformation into Relationship Marketing and one-to-one interaction for financial services, the airlines, and other industries.

While many companies made progress in building relationship brands, the new marketing was difficult to perfectly execute (at least economically). With the arrival of the Internet, a networked environment made it affordable for any company to have real relationships with customers for the first time in history. Now there are new demands on the organization to get the relationship right. As new technology increases the potential for meaningful and profitable interaction between company and customer, it also increases the potential for those interactions to fall short of meeting customer expectations.

In the mass marketing economy, the seller didn't really touch the buyer. Products were planned, created, and manufactured and then given to the company's Sales and Marketing arm to sell. Marketing in the era of mass distribution was done at arms' length to the customer.

In the networked environment, everything—every phone call, every contact with a company representative, every visit to the Web site—is customer-centric marketing. Every employee or agent of a company who touches a customer now must add value to the customer experience. And in the era of interactive relationship marketing, the long-term risks of negative touch also are immense.

While the Net part of the business might be exactly on the mark, and most of the customer orientation as well, the company might have one or two "weak links" that spoil the customer experience, which impacts the relationship brand and the future value of customer relationship.

Business travelers know all too well about these weak links: places where the relationship between the customer and the carrier breaks down.

For example, United Airlines can have a great Web site, creating ease for frequent flyers to monitor their awards. It can offer great deals and make it easy to buy E-tickets online. The check-in experience can be positive. The flight could be very pleasant; it might even leave on time. And the traveler might receive first-rate attention on board.

But if it takes 45 minutes to receive luggage, making you late for your son's soccer game, that one negative customer touch can negate the rest of the experience, leaving a negative impact on the brand itself.

Even attempts to improve customer experience can go awry if the focus is only on one part of the customer experience. To continue our airline example, while gate agents might have a fanatical focus on "on-time departure," passengers more likely are looking for on-time arrival! Misplaced focus can lead to misplaced investments in the wrong part of the process.

When customer experience becomes the touchstone for the brand, established companies are more exposed, even though they may have greater resources to leverage than Net-only companies. They often touch the customer many times in the course of a transaction.

This is one reason Web efforts like Expedia, Travelocity, and biztravel.com succeeded at first: they only touch the customer a few times, and most of those contacts are very easy to control, helping to ensure a positive overall experience. No traveler will blame Expedia or Travelocity if a flight is late or baggage is lost. Conversely, established companies who own the products or services themselves ultimately will come back into the driver's seat as they take more control of their company-customer relationships, as discussed earlier. For example, the airlines ultimately started selling their own tickets online and offering their own special promotions.

STRONG ONLINE LINKS

This presents both a challenge and an opportunity for established brands. A small part of the challenge is to create the best Web attraction possible for prospects and customers, then make sure that every time they "touch" the public, the experience adds value to the relationship. This is one of the reasons Amazon.com has been so successful at attracting repeat buyers.

At Amazon.com, a customer can enjoy browsing for books or music. Books are recommended, based on what that customer has purchased in the past. After a customer has made a purchase once, he or she is offered a one-click purchase. Amazon lets you know it has received your order, and creates a positive customer service environment. The company "remembers" the customer's address, credit card information, and shipping preference. The more a person visits, the easier it gets. Amazon continues to improve the customer experience every place it touches the customer.

In the physical world, organizations such as Ritz Carlton understand the concept of avoiding "weak links." At Ritz Carlton Hotels, employees are trained to resolve a customer's problem where it occurs. If a customer has a problem and contacts any employee on the premises, that employee takes ownership of the problem and personally seeks to get it resolved. With this approach, there are no weak links.

Of course, Ritz customers then expect the same level of service at the Web site, in addition to special promotions and the ability to purchase gift certificates, creating a positive end-to-end experience.

Conversely, if a company has weak links at too many contact points with customers, it might offset the lift obtained by a great Web site.

The opportunity for established companies to build online and offline complementary relationships, however, is huge if correctly executed. Rather than just using the Web as an extension of what they do in the physical world, retailers—to name only one example—have an opportunity to integrate the two, driving customers back and forth by creating value in each arena. Web opportunities can include online coupons to be cashed in at the physical store and in-store promotions can drive customers to the store's site.

Established companies that look at the Web as more than simply an additional distribution channel can create new opportunities. For example, anyone who purchases a CD player at Circuit City's Web site can pick it up at any Circuit City store. The physical and online businesses are integrated.

Many companies, such as Dell, Marriott, Hallmark, General Motors, and Terra have created positive online linkages to meet the expectations of their traditional customers.

Brick-and-mortar companies must use their Net efforts to identify and scrutinize every part of their value chain. This effort represents an opportunity to check and reevaluate every place the company touches a customer. For example,

- How is customer service?
- How are online feedback mechanisms used to show what is being done wrong?
- What other services can we provide?
- Which customers like which things that are done?
- What do its customers dislike most about dealing with the company?
- What is the company's weakest link?

DESTROYYOURBUSINESS.COM

As the large, established businesses realized the dramatic impact the interactive environment would have in their future, more dramatic steps were taken.

For example, GE Chairman Jack Welch brought the presidents of all GE divisions together and told them to embrace the Net and transform their business units using the Net. And he wasn't talking about selling more light bulbs online!

GE rallied around a phrase we introduced to GE called "destroyyourbusiness.com"[3] and started a series of meetings around every GE division on a global basis. The company came to realize that by rethinking old ways of doing things, it could create dramatic new efficiencies in its operations and streamline how it did business with all its customers, suppliers, and distributors, setting a standard for others to follow.

Another leading example is Ford, which decided to give a personal computer and Net access to all Ford employees, with the intent of creating a wired workforce more attuned to the world of information now made available to them and their families. Ford focused on creating a workforce with a hands-on understanding of the Net cconomy and it paid off.

REORGANIZING AROUND INFORMATION

The travel industry has been most profoundly affected by the emergence of the Net, and in the process of transforming itself has created a seemingly never-ending series of challenges and opportunities.

Travel has an enormous informational component. Think of the constant need to update data about airline schedules, fares, baggage, and passengers. It also has a daunting operational component in the physical world—the actual movement of planes, baggage, and people.

There are few industries more suited for a case study of how to organize a company to mesh its online and offline worlds—the place where IT and Marketing must forge a value-added relationship.

At Delta Airlines, when CEO Leo Mullin arrived in 1997, one of his first tasks was to attend a private, 3-hour meeting to look at where the company was in relation to Y2K.

"The basic conclusion was 'you can't get there from here,'"[4] Mullin says. "It was one of the most sobering meetings I've ever been to in my entire life."

The presentation to Mullin was made by Charlie Feld, who years earlier started the Feld Group to help companies that need radical transformation. He had been brought into Delta as Chief Information Officer (CIO), initially to help the company through Y2K.[5]

Mullin decided to take the "destroyyourbusiness.com" approach, and reset and recreate the future vision of the company:

> "Charlie mapped it out. He and I put a tremendous amount of emphasis on the technological advancements available and decided to spur the technological thinking around the world. We decided to throw out the old and bring in the new."

During that time, Y2K became priority no. 1 while customers became no. 2. During this time, "along comes the e-commerce revolution," says Mullin.

That revolution came to Delta in the form of Priceline.com, the Connecticut-based seller of name-your-own-price travel tickets, cars, and groceries.

"We looked at Priceline as either the ultimate opportunity or the ultimate threat to disintermediate our pricing structure," says Mullin. "That led to a substantial battle within the company." Delta ultimately allowed Priceline.com to sell Delta tickets in exchange for warrants for stock options in Priceline, the first airline to forge such a deal.

The company ultimately rallied behind the deal. After the initial public offering of Priceline, Delta made, on paper, more than $1 billion. It promptly cashed in $750 million of it.

This was part of the "wake-up" process within the company as to the new thinking needed for the Net economy. "People began to think in new and different ways. We had a new management team and a new appreciation of the role information could play," says Mullin.

So how did Delta get from there to here?

"We simplified the organization and placed accountability with the people. We lined up with the business context," says Feld, who also had been the CIO at Frito-Lay. He continues:

"In the 1960s and 1970s, IT worked for the Controller. In the 1980s, they worked for the functional heads, who saw technology as a productivity engine. In the 1990s, people started to realize stovepipes were killing them, so we moved to re-engineering and IT became the province of the senior staff."

"Now, IT is about business models and it has become inseparable from strategy."

So how did Delta make the business responsible for marketing and marketing responsible for business? It basically changed all the rules.

"We started with the premise, 'Wouldn't it be nice if you walked into the airline that was well run?' It would be very nice for a customer," says Feld.

"It was a physical event—eye contact—that mattered in the past, but as companies grow they tend to lose this. The simplicity is to look for the model, then get the physical and electronic events to be real-time feedback. You have to get the knowledge, then collapse the organization where you create the smallness of how a company grew up.

"At the beginning of the company, the computer was a person's mind.

"When you have a lot of scale, it's difficult to see from one end to the other. Scale is the enemy of knowledge. We had to say, 'What would the founder have done?' We had to find the brain of the founder."

Delta built one information system, and viewed anything that would connect to that system—personal computers, pagers, and hand-held devices—simply as appliances that connect to it. The company reorganized around information, with the view that access to the information for anyone, anywhere, anytime would enhance the customer experience and increase the value of the brand.

Since it had to deal with Y2K technological issues anyway, the Atlanta-based airline decided to create what Feld calls a "digital nervous system" of the entire airline.

"You have to strip away everything and act like a start-up. We said, 'If we were starting this company again today, what would we do? What would the founder have done?'

"We said what is the data model? We have customers, gates, and planes. We said as soon as an event happens, if there's a gate change, everybody who has 'subscribed' to the gate change application gets the information. It's the power of Real Time."

Delta previously had 15 different information "feeds" to various locations; when there was a gate change, people had to type in the information to pass it on. With its reorganization around information, the information flow became automatic.

Feld continues, "We said, as soon as there's a gate change, everybody has to know: the pilots, baggage handlers, passengers, flight attendants, and customers."

EMPLOYEE-CUSTOMER TOUCH

Of Delta Airline's 80,000 employees worldwide, including 35,000 pilots and 25,000 gate agents, about 65,000 touch a customer every day. This gives Delta thousands of daily opportunities to either enhance or damage the company-customer relationship.

When Mullin took over the helm of Delta, employee morale was at a relatively low point. As it rebuilt its insides around information to better serve its customers, the company also looked at how to involve its widely dispersed workforce in the effort.

"We wanted the employees to always be connected," says Feld. "There were three areas of information: what you need to do your job, the communications, and personal productivity."

Delta Airlines decided to give all its 80,000 employees a personal computer and Internet access, which it executed through People PC. "We placed no restrictions; they could be laptops, desktops, whatever. We told employees, 'We want you to become part of the digital economy,'" says Feld.

Adds Mullin:

"The wide-scale technological deployment gave our people a tremendous sense of pride. Making sure everybody is supplied with technology resource gives them a sense that they belong.

"We've encouraged our employees to let their children use it and I've had many cases of people coming up to me with tears in their eyes that we would do this."

Feld is proud that "employee satisfaction is now way up," and technology was cited as the number two reason. "There's a big connection between employee morale and customer service," he says.

CUSTOMER-COMPANY TOUCH

Delta has also not been untouched by the effects of e-commerce. "About 5 or 6 percent of our ticket sales moved to the Web, which brought $100 million to the bottom line." Feld continues:

> "You should be able to make a reservation online or through a cell phone, then walk up to a gate and swipe your card. This is the way all business travel will be. Any business traveler should never have to get in a line. When I get rebooked automatically because a flight connection is late, that information can go to my pager. When there's a gate change or change in flight time, Delta lets me know. We built all these new systems with the Net in mind."

The business traveler is a focus of Delta, since, as Mullin points out, 40 percent of Delta's revenue is derived from 10 percent of its customers. "That's a sophisticated group and technological group," he says.

Delta has built an information platform to change how customers interact with the company and has charged its entire organization with the challenge of implementing new marketing approaches to the customer.

The company also has Marketing and IT working hand-in-hand. "The trick here is to be able to let people innovate. The cycle time in typical IT process is too long," says Feld. "The way to a customer's heart is product innovation and low cost."

"We had a technological group attuned to marketing, because the technology and marketing are inextricably intertwined," says Mullin.

Feld adds:

> "The ability to innovate quickly is critical. If 90 percent of the technical code is written and the infrastructure is in place, then when an idea like smart cards comes along, you're within weeks of implementing.
>
> "Marketing is the keeper of the vision and the brand and dealing with customer reactions. Marketing is heavily involved in our work. It's the notion of no lines. Platinum membership is now about revenue, not miles. It's about having your high value customers segmented. We're turning this into an e-commerce customer-centric notion of business: 'I want to be paged,' 'I like this kind of food.' It's endless in this one-to-one relationship.
>
> "A lot of the environment you build has to come from the Marketing side. The brand is how the customer perceives you. It's the seat, it's the technology, the convenience. Branding is people knowing you. It's the experience.
>
> "Branding is information, like knowing if the plane is going to be on time."

During a hurricane in the Atlanta area, Delta gate agents brought up weather maps on their computer screens and turned the screens around so all the passengers could see them. According to Feld:

> "The brand is what you experience. You have to let customers tell you how they want to be treated. My relationship with Delta is a private one. It's with the database. It's about you telling me what you want, not about selling something.
>
> "There's the recognition that the brand is everything at Delta. It's all about brand and technology."

And Mullin, who says he "loves his job" heading Delta, says employees derive a new sense of satisfaction from their new access to information.

"There's now a sense of mission," says Mullin. The embracing of technology has been a crucial reason for Delta coming as far as it has in the industry. The culture of Delta has embraced it.

Delta took the approach that marketing and business were inseparable. It created an environment for information to be shared openly, realizing that Max-e-Marketing in the Net Future was about a one-to-one relationship and that everyone in the Delta "family" had to be active participants if it was going to improve their customers' experiences.

NEW POSITIONS REQUIRED

As companies look within their organizations for leadership of the e-business revolution, many companies have been turning to the CIO. Indeed, in one survey of CIOs, 40 percent said they were responsible for e-business.

However, it is interesting that only 10 percent believed they *should* be the one responsible.[6] Even technologists recognize the fact that though technology underlies much of the change required, the technical considerations are only one component of e-business.

In addition, while 33 percent of the CIOs said the CEO at their company was responsible, 30 percent believed it was the CEO who should take ultimate responsibility (the survey did not define whether they were the same 30 percent).

Most important, 40 percent thought a new position should be created within the enterprise. This finding supports the need for a rethinking of the role of both marketing and technology within the corporation. As e-commerce simply becomes a variation of commerce in general—or in some cases replaces it—the organization as a whole will begin to reflect the unique combination of demands it makes and skills it requires.

Many companies that initially created new positions, sometimes referred to as e-business czars, are beginning to make e-business part of the general makeup of company activities. By 2000, 70 percent of companies surveyed were melding their e-business strategies into existing business with existing management.[7]

The implications are basic. E-business units are accustomed to a rapidly changing marketplace. E-business units are accustomed to high employee turnover and tough recruiting demands. E-business units tend to be more comfortable with constant innovation and refining products and processes on the fly.

All of these traits may come as a shock to managers in more traditional areas of the company. As they begin working more closely than ever before with their e-business peers, it is not only technology and procedures that will come into conflict. It is cultural assumptions about the company's values, business, and very identity.

CREATING AN E-CATALYST AT FLEET

At New England–based Fleet Bank, which merged with BankBoston, the transformation came from the top. Recognizing that e-business would soon permeate the company, the CEO and COO not only named a person to head its e-business initiatives but also stayed personally involved on a regular basis.[8]

They named Brian Moynihan, Executive Vice President and Director of Corporate Strategy, and the executive who had run the bank's merger and acquisition activities, to the role of "e-catalyst."

Fleet decided a catalyst was better than a "czar," so that all managers would take ultimate responsibility. The catalyst and a group chaired by the CEO, which included the COO, President, CFO, CTO, and the head of Marketing, could be the driver. "When the top six people in the company get this involved, the company responds," says Moynihan.

"What we did in building dedicated Internet resource was create a core relationship platform," says Moynihan.

The group met every week and a half at the start, then had a 4-day meeting that involved all the business units. Now the panel meets every 3 to 4 weeks to help expedite hurdles, such as funding, as well as set priorities.

Fleet drove the responsibilities for Net initiatives through all their lines of business. It considered the idea of a stand-alone bank but rejected it. "From the customer's perspective, people wanted to get money anywhere they want, and you couldn't do that with online only," Moynihan continues.

"We had 25 smart Internet strategy people who work for me involved and we looked at the destroy-your-business model. We had people from the lines of business come and talk to the panel. With all the lines of business then working on it, we had 500 people dedicated to changing our business. They all took personal ownership.

"Ninety percent of this is about good marketing. These aren't technical problems. The role of Marketing in our company is on a meteoric rise. We have to make more people in the organization responsible for Marketing.

"The role of the CIO also has risen here, because the need to execute on time, on budget, is so acute now."

Whether the person leading the charge is called an e-czar or an e-catalyst, the CEO must look for a combination of skills that focus on external and internal issues that will be crucial for beating the competition in the Net Future.

THE NEW PARTNERSHIP

The promise of real-time responsiveness to customer needs and desires will drive a new partnership between IT and Marketing. While IT is key to the collection and internal dissemination of information, Marketing is key to determining what is collected, why it is needed, and what to do with it.

Once the information is collected and distributed, it is the marketing people who also help determine how it is used in product development, advertising and promotion, pricing, sales support, packaging, and distribution. IT, on the other hand, is still responsible for making sure that everything works and is cost effective.

As happened with Fleet, these two areas of responsibility will move up the value chain within the corporation as companies integrate their Net strategies with the rest of its operations.

Ironically, it was Marketing that was involved in the first stages of the commercial Net, before the interactive torch was passed to the IT departments. Perhaps even more ironically, it was IT that helped to orchestrate the inner weavings of technological platforms so that marketers could step back into the Net Future environment and take the business to new heights.

Several companies already take highly customer-centric approaches to organizing to meet customer needs, and have organized their structures to ensure that e-business is truly integrated with the rest of the organization. The effort at the Seagram Spirits and Wine Group was headed by Chief Marketing Officer Joseph Tripodi, the former CMO of MasterCard.[9] Tripodi says:

> "To ensure the appropriate strategy, we created a Resource Management Committee, which I chair. We have the CIO and leadership from Finance, Manufacturing, and Customer Service. What we do is prioritize activities to insure that the technology is being developed to meet our business needs."

At Nabisco Food Service, IT reports to Finance, while Marketing reports to the president.

"IT and marketing both are functional organizations," says Nabisco Food Service President Steven Rudnitsky.[10] He continues:

> "Most recognize IT as a means to an end. Functions like Marketing at Nabisco Food Service look at IT and

E-Business as a way to efficiently reach customers with new products. Our brand equity, as well as our IT capabilities are our strategic points of difference. IT has risen to the top of establishing viable points of differentiation against our competition."

MARKETING AND IT WORKING HAND IN HAND AT AAA

The American Automobile Association (AAA) comprises 86 affiliated clubs, with 1000 offices throughout the United States and Canada, all with autonomy for their geographical regions. With 37 million members in the United States, and more than 3 million in Canada, the clubs range from 10,000 to 3.5 million each. AAA offers everything from roadside assistance to travel planning; it also is the number one seller of American Express Travelers Cheques worldwide.

Each club has its own CEO, CIO, and support staffs, and each is allowed to control its own members' experiences, though the AAA brand is bolstered by nationwide advertising and marketing programs. The national office in Florida has a national CIO who leads technology initiatives, including setting a roadmap to provide direction for the members.

Not unlike many major corporations, the technical management found itself getting more and more involved in marketing and supporting the AAA members' experience.

To focus and align resources to maximize marketing, the association created the "Internet Coordinating Committee," comprising three executives: the managing director of associate systems, the managing director of marketing, and the managing director of publishing.[11] Ron Morehead, Managing Director, Systems Development, a

9-year AAA veteran responsible for all Internet-related systems says:

> "Marketing is going to help us communicate with our members online. They have a better view of what the member needs and are better at communicating. We need to communicate with real people and that's not the IT value added. The IT value added is in understanding the business needs and trying to make sure our staff really creates and runs what needs to be there. IT is more on the implementation side.
>
> "It works for us. We've had some experience where IT took the lead and we missed the mark, where we didn't hit the mark that we should have on our business side. This partnership with marketing gives us a much better chance to hit that mark. Nobody has all the answers.
>
> "With a small group of people working together, it works.
>
> "We meet for a few hours every other week and are moving that to weekly. We discuss new ideas people have presented to us and figure out what and how we can implement. We're the coordinators.
>
> "We've never had to escalate any higher than the committee. We deal with issues ranging from which keywords to register with the search engines to the look and feel of our presence and functionality development. We identify the best practices for the entire Association.
>
> "If push comes to shove, it depends in which area of expertise the issue falls under. Travel information and publishing is a big part of our business as well, so they're represented. Also, we're all friends, so

we're always frank with each other. That's the only way it will work.

"The biggest challenge our group faced and faces is sorting the wheat from the chaff. Vendors all want to tell us what they can do for us. Who to align with is a big issue.

"Marketing internally is sometimes more difficult than marketing externally, because there are a lot of good ideas of where the initiative should be going. Clubs might have different priorities and resources based on size. Another issue is that people expect things to be perfect out of the box because that's the way it has been. We're now telling people to expect more of a tradeoff. If development speed is the priority, this probably won't be perfect initially. We've told our clubs we're going to do things that may not totally meet their expectations.

"We have some national standards and some brand standards. Continuity is one of our biggest challenges. We must manage our brand from a national perspective, but each club is closer to the customer. As a group, we really know the local market. We have 86 clubs with a lot of local knowledge. That's a strength and a weakness.

"IT and Marketing is *the* partnership to bring it all together, because it's the customer experience that will matter the most in the future."

COMBINING IT AND MARKETING TO CREATE VALUE

Meshing IT and Marketing can represent a formidable challenge. The two must work hand in glove for the customer experience to be consistently satisfying. Yet, the two cultures have responsibilities and ways of creating value for both the organization and the customer that are very different.

Each has its own way of creating value for the company and ultimately the customer. Some of the factors involved in each are shown in Figure 7.1.

TECHNOLOGY PLATFORMS/PRODUCT PLATFORMS

Because IT is responsible for developing and maintaining technological standards, the standardization that leads to cost efficiencies is often a top priority. That can represent a problem for marketers who are focused on trying to market offerings in such a way that the company becomes an innovation leader within the industry. The Net Marketing requires that each customer be treated in as personalized a way as possible. We have presented some examples of infrastructure software applications and information technology that can help companies achieve both cost efficiencies and customized customer experiences (see Imperative 6).

INFRASTRUCTURE AS BRAND

In the Net economy, Internet infrastructure is the brand platform.

One of the first pioneers to recognize the communications potential of the Internet, even before it became commercial, is G. M. O'Connell, Chairman of Modem Media. He worked with *Fortune 500* companies as they moved through all five steps of the Net evolution process. He was involved in helping Delta Airlines work through its interactive strategy.

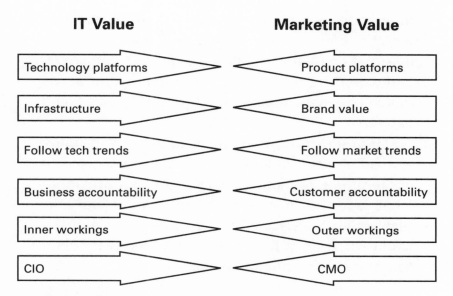

FIGURE 7.1 The IT and Marketing culture bring complementary value to Max-e-Marketing.

With the recognition that e-business is no longer a separate function but an outgrowth of the business as a whole has come a realization that operational performance is the new metric of marketing success.[12]

However, that realization has led to conflict between the two functional areas. O'Connell sees it this way:

"Everybody wants to be customer-centric now. I mean, who doesn't want that? The question is, can you put the infrastructure in place to support it? You've got to have great marketing concepts, but unless you have the ability to execute, the concepts may do more harm than good.

"Look at the airlines' advertising right now. It essentially says, 'We're going to try to do what you want us to do.' In the future it won't be about trying. It will be about travelers getting information in real time about everything involving their interactions with the company—for example, getting accurate information on a wireless device about flight arrival and departure times and having their experiences match or exceed their expectations of what's going to happen.

"If you're not providing true value and utility instead of just messaging, you won't be successful in the future. Marketing is going to be more about what you do and less about what you say. Messaging built some of the great brands of the twentieth century. But the new commodity is advertising; the differentiator will be service.

"Most of the money in interactive marketing is not being spent on advertising. Right now the lion's share of the money is being spent on capabilities that a company thinks it wants to be able to deliver to the customer. That's the razor. The blades will be in delivery of the relevant information that enables a customer to use those services in a customer-centric way.

"Right now CRM stands for "customer relationship management." It should stand for "company relationship management." The rules are being written by the customer. When a company's information systems or Web site configures itself to the customer, the customer has the management of the relationship to the company instead of the other way around. A company will only be successful if it allows the customer to manage it instead of managing the customer.

"The question is, who calls the shots when the customer is this directly connected to the company's operational side? Is it marketing or is it IT? Most of our clients have had difficulty in getting marketing and IT to work together. Marketing tries to outline what needs to be done; IT says that (1) marketing doesn't write requirements, (2) marketing writes requirements that don't have any basis in reality, or (3) marketing has to get in line behind other projects that need to be implemented.

"IT requires strong leadership and follow-through. The CEOs have generally stepped in pretty quickly and demonstrated that they won't tolerate noncooperation."

As previously discussed, getting others to do the work they can do better is essential in the Net Future. Getting Marketing and IT departments and leaders to work together will be just as essential.

TECH TRENDS/MARKET TRENDS

IT departments often cope with emerging technologies that can make a project obsolete even before it's completely installed. If kept informed about the marketing department's concerns, they can also be the first to recognize new technologies that can help to solve marketing challenges.

Marketing departments face a similar challenge: a rapidly changing market environment and competitive pressures can demand new offerings of products and services much more rapidly than ever before. If kept informed about new ways to automate customer relations and use database information, they can turn the new opportunities into value-added customer experiences.

BUSINESS ACCOUNTABILITY/ MARKETING ACCOUNTABILITY

Because IT budgets often represent such a large portion of a company's overall costs, IT is often under the direct control of the chief financial officer, who is responsible for making sure spending is in line with revenue. A CIO is often judged as much on cost-containment efforts as on any technological achievements. Marketing, however, is largely rewarded based on increasing market share, and increasing revenues often means spending money.

These two drivers—cost containment and funding new marketing efforts—do not have to be in conflict if management thinks strategically and sets priorities with one eye on present performances and the other eye on the future value of the company's customer or client relationships.

INTERNAL FOCUS/EXTERNAL FOCUS

IT is like an iceberg; much of its work is out of sight, sunken behind a corporate firewall and may be invisible even within the corporation. Marketing's focus is outward, on interaction with customers and competitors. The difference means that each department gets its information about the Enterprise's success or failure from different sources. That difference in information sources can lead to confusion about the company's direction and priorities.

The 51 percent rule demands that IT adopt more of marketing's outward focus. Doing so will help the company to align its technology more closely with its market goals. However, it will not be an easy paradigm to change.

IT has traditionally been charged with protecting the company's data. In some cases, that has led to extreme protectiveness about access to information, even within the company. At a time when hackers abound, that concern has never been more justified.

The challenge is to find ways to facilitate the acquisition and circulation of more outside information while maintaining the integrity of sensitive material. The way Delta found it could offer accurate information directly to customers about weather-related flight delays is an example of learning to rethink just how sensitive some information is, and how it can be put to better use.

MORE THAN MARKETING AND TECHNOLOGY

Sometimes it's not enough just to get Marketing and IT to work together, no matter how harmoniously. It also requires support from the top, as well as a genuine business understanding of the true competition realities and strategic objectives of the company.

For example, when Chicago-based Bank One launched Wingspan, the "bank without branches," it assembled a 20-person internal strike team to get it off the ground.[13] The group was given a mere 16 weeks to launch the new bank.

Terry Ransford had a background in Sales and Sales Management before moving to IT, ultimately becoming CIO of Roney & Co., a Michigan-based division of Bank One. Ransford was subsequently named to the launch team as President and CEO of Wingspan Investment Services. Ransford says:

> "Our 16-week approach had more to do with beating Citibank to market. The thinking was that being first would be the winning proposition, since no one had a national presence for banking online.

Bank One, which had grown largely by acquisitions, had multiple pricing structures in different states as well as seven separate legacy banking computer systems. The launch team was given the ability to start from scratch, building what was necessary, as long as it could be accomplished within the given timeframe. Ransford continues:

> "We decided that to be quick and nimble there was too much legacy and too much baggage to build on what we had. We were told there were no rules, just go do what you need to do to beat the competition. Time to market was everything."

The internal team comprised employees from First USA as well as Bank One, from Marketing, Systems, Brokerage, and Banking.

"Marketing drove it," says Ransford, noting First USA's heritage of being the first to do online approval of credit cards in a large-scale way.

"Wingspan was all about customer acquisition. We looked at how we could use technology to extend the marketing initiatives."

Although Wingspan gained 100,000 accounts in 7 months, Ransford says the value proposition simply wasn't compelling enough.

> "We had good marketing, good systems, but nobody understood the business. People would have to give up normal banking to do this. They didn't understand the business well enough.
>
> "When you go to a bank, you want a checking account, you fill out a form. If you want a credit card, you fill out another form. If you want a savings

account, you fill out another form. You keep repeating the same information on each form.

"At Wingspan, we had one application; we had that down. But no one spent any time on 'How do you get money into the bank account?' E*Trade bought an ATM network because they understood this was a big issue.

"Wingspan did not offer joint accounts, so the decision process was only single name because of the company's credit-card heritage," says Ransford, noting that credit card acquisition strategy is always focused on one individual, not a couple.

"The drivers were Marketing and IT. There should have been a third leg to the stool, or a business person who understood technology. Marketing can't drive the business and IT can't drive the business, but someone has to come up with the compelling value proposition.

"Effective decisions are made when all the parties are at the table. You need to understand the business implications and the Marketing implications. IT and Marketing can provide the third leg if you have the right people. IT and Marketing is a logical partnership. Wingspan did a lot more right than it did wrong.

"In the final analysis, we're in a bulk commodity business. A bank's a bank. It's a gigantic business without a value proposition."

As Bank One absorbed Wingspan back into the core Bank One operations, leveraging the lessons learned, Ransford moved on to become Senior Vice President and Director of E-Commerce at Northern Trust, a major regional bank also headquartered in Chicago.

Ironically, Northern Trust set about the same launch timeframe for its Internet banking transformation, acquiring team members from various disciplines inside and outside the bank.

The chairman appointed an e-commerce "czar," who reported directly to him.

"Time to market here has to do with meeting our customers' expectations," says Ransford, who notes that the bank focuses heavily on "not letting our customers down."

At Northern Trust, Ransford has two offices, one in the building where Marketing is housed. The other is in another building where the entire Interactive team makes its home, and where he is physically 8 feet from the CIO. With a regular shuttle of company buses between buildings that are 8 minutes apart, Ransford goes back and forth between meetings in each building all day. He says:

> "The IT guys with us are happy to get away because this stuff is sexy and it's on the edge, while the big iron is dusty. This is all new stuff.
>
> "It used to be that Marketing people would meet and then tell IT what they want and then say they didn't get it. Marketing is now involved in the user testing and we put IT and Marketing in the same meetings.
>
> "The Marketing people are forced to understand what some of the technology can do. This CRM and database stuff is finally letting them do what they all wanted to do. They can now segment and analyze. We can now judge who's getting the messages. We have click-through rates. The Marketing guys are all over that. The IT guys appreciate that what they do is greatly desired.

"Marketing was largely intuitive. But now Marketing can get real data and see customer behavior. It's all about customer acquisition cost and net present value. Now we can say we should spend on this customer because we can see the net present value of the account is considerably higher than the customer acquisition cost.

"The interest of Marketing and Technology are now one and the same. When you add the Net business it costs a lot. You need to be able to show a return on my dollars invested."

So is Terry Ransford considered Marketing or IT? "I don't really know. I guess I'm now more of a business line guy."

THE NEW INTEGRATION

To be a Max-e-Marketer, a business must be more tightly integrated than ever before if it is to create a total relationship brand. Marketing will have to permeate the organization, ensuring that it is directed toward meaningful value-added experiences in everything done *to*, *for*, and *with* the customer.

With the transition to full involvement in the Net Future come new responsibilities, for both the marketing department and the entire organization. True understanding and focus on the escalating needs of connected customers requires empowering everyone to solve customer problems on their own authority more than ever before.

Business objectives often are clearly articulated within and throughout companies. But the actual real-time implementation and execution around changing customer demands has been difficult and sometimes impossible to execute. Instability is resisted by technologists, and real-time data by its very nature increases the degree of instability in the way the Enterprise works.

As the rapid pace of innovation continues, management will have to use real-time information to drive all aspects of the business. Alignments with external partners—and even, at times, with competitors—are an ongoing fact of life to prevent being overwhelmed by the torrent of new technology every business faces.

There is also an internal alignment taking place. More and more CEOs are getting personally involved in driving the e-business initiatives of their companies, as they see the profound implications of the new networked environment.

They are coming to realize that it is all about lasting customer relationships that create the future value of the enterprise. Perception of the advertising-supported brand is, if anything, more important than ever in today's fiercely competitive environment. But it no longer is enough alone to ensure the future well-being of the company.

The power of the brand reflects the enduring quality of the customer experience, as interactive relationships enable the customer to take the measure of the company day in and day out.

THE NEW NECESSITY—LIVING WITH CONSTANT INNOVATION

If a business is to be truly customer-focused, every part of the company must be constantly aware of what is being done in relation to creating a better customer experience. The guy on the loading dock, the purchasing officer, the data-entry clerk, the programmer—all are potential sources of new ideas and feedback for the company. Peter Lynch, the famed former mutual fund manager for Fidelity Investments, used to encourage individual investors to invest in what they knew, to use their everyday experiences to produce investment ideas. Every employee in a company can follow the same precept. And with the connective power of the Internet, the potential input stream is—or should be—limitless.

INFORMATION TECHNOLOGY *IS* WHAT THE BUSINESS IS ABOUT

Every company is in two industries: its own and information technology. It is not only because the information flow is so critical to the understanding of the customer and the distribution of goods and services. It is also so because companies have made new businesses out of information technology that solves their own problems and made fortunes marketing it to their competitors.

KEEP YOUR ANTENNAE OUT

This can't be stressed enough. A company should make sure it's taking in and circulating at least as much information from the external world as it is exporting from inside the company. It's the only way to stay on top of the changes that prompt innovation.

In the end, for companies who are able to implement the kind of close-knit connection between technology and marketing that Max-e-Marketing success demands, there will be a huge return on the IT investment. Not only will marketing efforts be enhanced but also the company's ability to attract the best and brightest employees will get a boost. Everyone wants to be with a company on the cutting edge of new technology applications.

This seventh imperative in many ways underlies all the rest. Unless it becomes a core value of the business, management will have difficulty implementing the other six. But if IT and Marketing innovators can surmount the challenges involved and build the necessary cultural bridges, both the company and the individuals within it will be winners.

NOTES

1. First identified by the author in *Net Future*, New York: McGraw-Hill, 1999.
2. Net Future Institute survey of 2500 business executives in 1500 companies in 32 countries.
3. The term "destroyyourbusiness.com" was introduced to GE executives in a lecture given by one of the authors.
4. Based on the authors' interview with Delta CEO Leo Mullin.
5. The following is based on the authors' interviews with Charlie Feld. Numerous Delta executives were also interviewed.
6. The statistics in this and the following paragraphs are based on a survey conducted at a *Business Week* CIO conference in New York, which was chaired by the author.
7. Net Future Institute survey of 2500 business executives in 1500 companies in 32 countries.
8. The following is based on the authors' interviews with Brian Moynihan, Executive Vice President and Director of Corporate Strategy and the E-Catalyst at Fleet.
9. Based on the authors' interview with Seagram Chief Marketing Officer Joseph Tripodi.
10. Based on the authors' interview with Nabisco Food Service President Steven Rudnitsky.
11. The following is based on the authors' interview with Ron Morehead, Managing Director, Systems Development at AAA.
12. The following is based on the authors' interviews with G. M. O'Connell, Modem Media Chairman.
13. The following is based on the authors' interviews with Terry Ransford, former President and CEO of Wingspan Investment Services.

WHERE DO YOU GO FROM HERE?

The future isn't what it used to be. You no longer must wait for it to arrive. We live and do business in a Net Future that is all around us. Those companies that first identify "what will be" while taking advantage of "what is" are the Max-e-Marketing winners.

A NEW MODEL FOR MEASURING BRAND VALUE

Three-year planning used to be a business standard, but now in response to the latest turn in technology or shifting customer priorities, the smartest managers often set and implement a new strategic direction in months rather than years.

As every business is thrust into a direct, interactive relationship with end-user customers, there is a steady flow of real-time feedback from the marketplace. Any company with a decision-making process that ignores it—or doesn't use it effectively— will be at a competitive disadvantage.

You must be constantly asking: "What are we doing to build future value? What are we doing to enhance existing customer relationships? How quickly are we adapting to the latest changes in the marketplace?"

How you now create an environment for growth and build future value differs from the traditional formula. (See the table.)

Relationship Value Drivers

Traditional Marketing	New Marketing Formula
$BV = p + q$	$BV = e + p + q$

Note: BV = brand value, p = brand perception, and q = quality of the offering, e = brand experience.

How do you add to your brand equity in the new networked business scene? First and foremost is the need for remaining flexible in order to make the most of shifting opportunities and technological change. The Net Future environment means that every company, no matter what the industry, is now in more direct contact with its customers than ever before. That means a greater proportion of the brand value than ever before will come from the customer's varied interactions with the entire company—direct experience.

As a result, the new formula for success becomes:

Brand value = brand experience + brand perception + quality of offering

or

$$BV = e + p + q$$

This equation can be applied not just to an individual customer but also to the company's relationship with its customers as a whole. On a macro level, it reflects the fact that in planning strategic acquisitions or joint ventures, CFOs cannot afford to ignore or undervalue the intangibles that each party brings to the table, such as customer goodwill and the databases that reflect what the company knows about its customers. In the Net Future, the intangible, information-based assets are considered as physical assets or transaction-based assets such as accounts receivable.

In the New Future, unlocking the future value of the relationship with your customers is the primary focus of the seven Max-e-Marketing imperatives. The enterprise will need to encourage its managers and employees to understand this model for growing the enterprise and to provide incentives for employees to create value in their day-to-day interactions with customers.

The Max-e-Marketing approach demands that the entire organization not only adopt a customer-centric perspective but also that it reinvent itself structurally so that linking brand value and relationship value becomes hard-wired into its everyday operations.

COMPETING ON CONNECTION

As stated at the beginning of this book, the new marketing is about relationships, experiences, and the value of both in terms of sales and profits.

Max-e-Marketing in the Net Future involves moving from a transaction-based relationship to an ongoing, connection-based relationship that includes all aspects of customer contact. It is that relationship that is the new brand equity.

If you can emerge as the dominant relationship player in your field, you may be perceived as operating on an entirely different plane from your competitors. If you can become the Dell of your field, you are competing not on price or even product, but on connection.

Businesses will find that they can achieve breakthrough strategies in the Net Future by using what they know to drive what they do. They often begin by being opportunistic, by building strategies that help them exploit opportunities for their core business, based on what they know.

To be successful, businesses will constantly re-evaluate strategies, updating them based on real-time knowledge. New business opportunities will increasingly enhance strategic advantage.

This is how Meredith Corporation is building a breakthrough strategy.[1] Meredith started opportunistically, by building a database of consumer information to better target customers for its publications. It then leveraged that consumer information to help target messages for advertising clients. It subsequently became the expert on consumers and how they buy products.

Now Meredith knows more about how consumers buy its advertisers' products than its advertisers do.

GETTING STARTED WITH THE 7 MAX-E-MARKETING IMPERATIVES

The first step in implementing *Max-e-Marketing in the Net Future* is to ask a lot of questions about not only your current marketing efforts but also about your organization's ability to adapt to the new customer demands of the new Net economy. Regardless of whether you are the Marketing Director, the Customer Relationship Manager, the CIO, or the CEO, you will need to be more aware than ever before of how the entire organization touches every customer.

Here are suggested starting points for making an assessment of which Max-e-Marketing imperatives might best benefit your company:

1. Review the four A's.
   - *Addressability*: What new avenues for identfying known customers are opening up as a result of the new information technology?
   - *Accountability*: How do you monitor what's working and what's not?
   - *Affordability*: Are you maximizing the potential of automated customer care software to reduce cost?
   - *Accessibility*: How are you taking advantage of the new channels for customer contact online and offline? How do you decide what customer information is most important?

2. Audit your existing Relationship Brand.
   - Where are the weak links in your contacts with prospects and customers?
   - What do you do to build customer bonding experiences?
   - What do you do to stimulate customer loyalty?

3. Assess what you already know.
   - How close are you to achieving the 51 percent rule?
   - How many individual data points do you have on each customer?
   - What existing customer touch points offer possibilities for capturing useful information, and are they being actualized?
   - How do you reward customers for giving you valuable information, both initially and ongoing?
   - What Net Future customer care technologies are you already using in your marketing efforts? Are you exploiting them to the fullest?

4. Decide what else you need to know.
   - What do you need to know to cross-sell, upsell, and new-sell your customers more effectively?
   - How do you need to structure the organization to get the first-mover advantage and proceed profitably?
   - How can you use existing customers to help you find other customers?
   - What information-gathering efforts can be out-sourced to specialists to leverage their expertise?

5. Decide how you'll use the information.
   - How will you use customer data to drive the development of new offerings? To improve customer service? Distribution? Marketing?
   - How will you disseminate vital customer information throughout the company?
   - How will you totally protect customer privacy?

6. Organize so that Marketing and IT are on the same page.
   - Who currently makes decisions about prioritizing the implementation of new technologies?
   - How do you create a structure that facilitates cooperation in the decision-making process?
   - What mechanisms are in place to ensure that Marketing and IT have compatible goals and strategies?
   - How do Marketing and IT join forces to make the best possible use of customer data?

As we have noted throughout this book, maximizing sales and profits through Max-e-Marketing requires a focus on the future value of established relationships while at the same time blurring the lines between Marketing and Information Technology. To achieve this kind of integrated approach to customer relationship management (CRM), companies must be willing to rethink their assumptions about who is responsible for what. In many ways, the seventh imperative—"Make Marketing Responsible for Business and Business Responsible for Marketing"—underlies all the others.

It doesn't mean that marketers will be writing code, or that programmers will suddenly be expected to create brochures. However, marketers will need to be aware of the profound changes technology is bringing to the many ways in which the business can now interact with customers. And technologists who understand the demands of the marketplace and how making their special know-how accessible increasingly drives the way the company does business.

We recognize that some of the changes we envision may conflict with long-established marketing and management rules. However, it was only a few years ago that businesses viewed the Net as a nice place to post a corporate brochure. The changes that have been wrought since then have already profoundly altered the nature of business. What comes next is certain to be just as dramatic.

We wish you good luck with your own Max-e-Marketing experimentation and rule breaking innovations as you respond to the twists and turns of the Net Future! In this amazing new interconnected world in which we live and work, we all will be learning from one another in creating the best possible Net Future outcomes.

NOTE

1. Based on the authors' interviews with Laurence Bunin, CEO of Handshake Dynamics, Meredith's strategy consultant.

URL Listing

Company	URL
AAA	www.aaa.com
AAdvantage	www.aadvantage.com
Abilitec	www.abilitec.com
About.com	www.about.com
Ace Hardware	www.acehardware.com
Acxiom	www.acxiom.com
AdAge	www.adage.com
AdAlive	www.adalive.com
Amazon	www.amazon.com
American Airlines	www.aa.com
American Express	www.americanexpress.com
AOL	www.aol.com
Ariba	www.ariba.com
Arthur Andersen	www.arthurandersen.com
Asimba.com	www.asimba.com
AT&T	www.att.com
Auto-by-Tel	www.autobytel.com
Aveo	www.aveo.com
Bally Fitness	www.ballyfitness.com

Company	URL
Bank of Montreal	www.bmo.com
Bank One	www.bankone.com
BankRate	www.bankrate.com
Barnesandnoble.com	www.bn.com
Baskin Robbins	www.baskinrobbins.com
biztravel.com	www.biztravel.com
BMG	www.bmg.com
Boots	www.boots.co.uk
Borders.com	www.borders.com
Bradesco	www.bradesco.com
Brightware	www.brightware.com
Burger King	www.burgerking.com
Business Week	www.businessweek.com
C/NET	www.cnet.com
Cargill	www.cargill.com
Chevron Corp.	www.chevron.com
Chrysler	www.chrysler.com
Circuit City	www.circuitcity.com
ClickAction	www.clickaction.com
CMGI	www.cmgi.com
CNBC	www.cnbc.com
CNN	www.cnn.com
Coke	www.coke.com
Collectibles.com	www.collectibles.com
Compaq	www.compaq.com
CompUSA	www.compusa.com

Company	URL
CyberGold	www.cybergold.com
Cyberhomes.com	www.cyberhomes.com
Dell	www.dell.com
Deloitte Consulting	www.deloitte.com
Delta	www.delta.com
Digital Impact	www.digitalimpact.com
Disney	www.disney.com
Dunkin' Donuts	www.dunkindonuts.com
E*Trade	www.etrade.com
E.piphany	www.epiphany.com
E-bay	www.ebay.com
E-Dialog	www.edialog.com
eGain	www.egain.com
Egg	www.egg.com
Enamics	www.enamics.com
Encirq	www.encirq.com
EntryPoint	www.entrypoint.com
Envera (oil exchange)	www.envera.com
Epidemic.com	www.epidemic.com
Epsilon	www.epsilon.com
Expedia	www.expedia.com
Fair Isaac & Co.	www.fairisaac.com
Favemail	www.favemail.com
Federal Express	www.fedex.com
Fidelity Investments	www.fidelity.com
Firestone	www.firestone.com

Company	URL
First Tuesday.com	www.firsttuesday.com
First USA	www.firstusa.com
Fleet Boston Financial	www.fleet.com
Flo Network	www.flonetwork.com
Florists Transworld Delivery	www.ftd.com
Food.com	www.food.com
Forbes	www.forbes.com
Ford Motor Company	www.ford.com
FreeSamples.com	www.freesamples.com
Frito-Lay	www.fritolay.com
Frontstep	www.frontstep.com
Garden.com	www.garden.com
Gateway	www.gateway.com
Gazooba.com	www.gazooba.com
GE Power Systems	www.gepower.com
General Electric	www.ge.com
General Motors	www.gm.com
Genuity	www.genuity.com
Gizmoz	www.gizmoz.com
Glaxo SmithKline	www.glaxosmithkline.com
Gomez	www.gomez.com
Handshake Dynamics	www.handshakedynamics.com
Harte-Hanks	www.hartehanks.com
Hewlett-Packard	www.hp.com
Hyatt	www.hyatt.com
IBM	www.ibm.com
IDG Books	www.idgbooks.com

Company	URL
IHRSA	www.ihrsa.com
ImproveNet	www.improvenet.com
Intel	www.intel.com
Internet Capital Group	www.internetcapital.com
iSKY	www.isky.com
iUniverse	www.iuniverse.com
iWon.com	www.iwon.com
JC Penney	www.jcpenney.com
J.C. Whitney	www.jcwhitney.com
John Deere	www.johndeere.com
Kelloggs	www.kelloggs.com
KitchenAid	www.kitchenaid.com
Kraft	www.kraft.com
L90	www.L90.com
Lands' End	www.landsend.com
Levi Strauss	www.levistrauss.com
Live Person	www.liveperson.com
LLBean	www.llbean.com
Marks and Spenser	www.marks-and-spenser.co.uk
MasterCard	www.mastercard.com
Mattel	www.mattel.com
Maytag	www.maytag.com
McCann Relationship Marketing	www.mrmworldwide.com
McDonald's	www.mcdonalds.com
MCI	www.mci.com
McKinsey	www.mckinsey.com

Company	URL
Mercedes-Benz	www.mercedes.com
Meredith	www.meredith.com
Metro Mail	www.metromail.com
MindArrow Systems	www.mindarrow.com
Modem Media	www.modemmedia.com
More.com	www.more.com
MyPoints.com	www.mypoints.com
Nabisco	www.nabisco.com
National Association of Realtors	www.realtor.com
Naviant	www.naviant.com
Neoforma.com	www.neoforma.com
Net Creations	www.netcreations.com
Net Future Institute	www.netfutureinstitute.com
Net Perceptions	www.netperceptions.com
Netcentives	www.netcentives.com
NetClerk	www.netclerk.com
NetPulse (San Francisco)	www.netpulse.com
Netscape	www.netscape.com
New York Stock Exchange	www.nyse.com
NFO	www.nfo.com
Nike	www.nike.com
OAG	www.oag.com
Office Depot	www.officedepot.com
Oracle	www.oracle.com
Owners.com	www.owners.com
p-co.com	www.p-co.com

Company	URL
PeopleSoft	www.peoplesoft.com
Pepsi	www.pepsi.com
Perks.com	www.perks.com
Pets.com	www.pets.com
PricewaterhouseCooper	www.pwcglobal.com
Priceline	www.priceline.com
Procter & Gamble	www.pg.com
Promotions.com	www.promotions.com
Quest	www.quest.com
RealTime Media Inc.	www.realtimemedia.com
Reflect.com	www.reflect.com
Ritz-Carlton	www.ritzcarlton.com
Safeway	www.safeway.com
SAP	www.sap.com
SAS	www.sas.com
Sears	www.sears.com
ServiceMagic.com	www.servicemagic.com
Seven-Eleven	www.seveneleven.com
Smile	www.smile.co.uk
Sony	www.sony.com
Speednews	www.speednews.com
Staples	www.staples.com
Sweepsclub.com	www.sweepsclub.com
Sysco	www.sysco.com
TellThemNow.com	www.tellthemnow.com
Tesco	www.tesco.co.uk
The Associates	www.theassociates.com

Company	URL
The Gap	www.gap.com
Thomas Cook Holdings	www.thomascook.co.uk
Togo's	www.togos.com
Tower Records	www.towerrecords.com
Travelocity	www.travelocity.com
Tyson Foods	www.tyson.com
United Airlines	www.united.com
USA Today	www.usatoday.com
UserTrends	www.usertrends.com
Verizon	www.verizon.com
VHA inc.	www.vha.com
Victoria's Secret	www.victoriassecret.com
Virgin	www.virgin.com
Wal-Mart	www.walmart.com
Westin, The	www.westin.com
Wingspan Bank	www.wingspan.com
Wired Magazine	www.wired.com
Xerox	www.xerox.com
zoho.com	www.zoho.com

Glossary

Brand experience   A customer's experience of a satisfaction with a product, the interactive contact experience with the company, and the opinions of others in multiple contexts over time. (See Imperative 6.)

Brand value   A product of brand equity plus relationship equity.

Careware   The software and hardware systems that integrate your customer database with your marketing campaigns and subsequent customer interactions, especially those that provide ongoing customer support. (See Imperative 6.)

E-marketplace   A digital commerce platform where companies can aggregate their suppliers, or businesses can combine their electronic procurement processes.

Electronic customer relationship management (eCRM) Customer resources conducted electronically.

51 percent rule   At least 51 percent of a company's communication should come from the customer and be circulated throughout the company.

Four A's   The four factors that determine direct marketing success in the Net Future. They are addressability, accountability, affordability, and accessibility. (See New Millennium! New Networked Economy! New Marketing Imperatives!)

Integrated eCRM   Integrating offline and online customer relationship management.

Max-e-Marketing   Maximizing sales and profits by applying effective interactions with known prospects and customers across all touch points and all communication channels.

Max-i-Marketing   A way to maximize sales and profits by selective interaction and involvement with identified prospects and customers.

Offering   A combination of product and service that creates an integrated answer to a customer's needs. (See Imperative 2.)

P911   Code typed in by kids on AOL chat rooms to alert their peers that a parent has entered the room. (See Imperative 5.)

Team sourcing   Outsourcing in which company and vendor become so tightly linked that the outsourced capability is inextricably tied to the parent company. (See Imperative 4.)

Verb branding   Developing a trademark or brand name into a verb that represents the company's brand image. It can be a strong indicator of the true nature of a company's business. (See Imperative 5.)

Index

About the Authors

Stan Rapp is Chairman and CEO of McCann Relationship Marketing (MRM), Worldwide, and a member of the Board of McCann-Erickson WorldGroup. MRM is a global leader in CRM marketing practices with offices in 33 countries. Rapp is a member of the Hall of Fame of the Direct Marketing Association and was recently honored by *Advertising Age* magazine and the Advertising Club of New York for his central role in shaping the history of advertising in the twentieth century. The five books co-authored by Stan Rapp and Tom Collins first predicted and then illuminated the shift from mass marketing to individualized marketing.

Chuck Martin, a popular online publisher, lecturer, marketer, and author, is chairman and CEO of Net Future Institute, a U.S.-based think tank focusing on the future of the Internet and e-business. He has been a journalist at five daily newspapers and has been editor-in-chief of four national magazines. He was Associate Publisher of *Information Week* and was founding Publisher of *Interactive Age*. Most recently, he was Vice President of Publishing and Advertising at IBM. He is the author of *The New York Times* Business best-seller, *The Digital Estate*, and also, *Net Future*.